A HEROINE'S JOURNEY

by
Helene K. Joy

WHOLLY LIFE CENTER (U.C.C.)

P.O. Box 1703   Aptos, CA 95001

For my children

and for my sisters everywhere
who find my Journey empowering.

ACKNOWLEDGMENTS

This book came to birth with the encouragement of a loving team of midwives: Doret Kollerer of Chabot College helped me "find my voice" as a writer and so began the task. Author and friend, Eva Fugitt, read my manuscript and gave inspiration and practical advice. My spiritual sisters, Ann Elliott and Lenora Huett, lent their support at crucial stages of this tale's evolution. My own family "matriarchy"—consisting of my daughter, "Lynn," my sister, "Carrie," and her daughters, my nieces—assured me of the value of my story by their enthusiastic appreciation for its relevance to their lives. I especially thank "Lynn," who brought loving patience and great wisdom to her many chapter-by-chapter suggestions.

My thanks to my son, "Clark," who expressed his confidence in me as a writer by giving me the gift of a Macintosh computer for this book, and patiently, lovingly teaching me to use it. My pastor-friends, "John and Anna," lent their encouragement in many ways. And, most of all, without the constant support of my spiritual brother, "William," this tale could not have been told.

The spirit of Helen M. Luke shines through much of my story, for she has been a Wise Woman revealing to me the depths of my own woman-hunger and illuminating my path. She has my unbounded gratitude for her inspiration as a writer, a counselor and as a woman, and for permission to quote from her self-published booklet: *The Way of Woman, Ancient and Modern.*

I also gratefully acknowledge permission to quote from the following works by their respective publishers:

The Kingdom Within: A Study of the Inner Meaning of Jesus' Sayings by John A. Sanford (J. B. Lippincott Co.), copyright 1970 by John A. Sanford. Selections used by permission of Harper & Row, Publishers, Inc.

Goddesses In Everywoman: A New Psychology of Women by Jean Shinoda Bolen, M.D. Copyright 1984 by Jean Shinoda Bolen.. Selections used by permission of Harper & Row, Publishers, Inc.

Becoming Woman by Penelope Washbourn. Copyright 1977 by Penelope Washbourn. Selections used by permission of Harper & Row, Publishers, Inc.

CONTENTS

PREFACE

A friend surprised me recently with these words: "You're a living symbol of the heroine on her journey. When I look at you I feel like I'm beholding that timeless archetype[1] in flesh and blood."

Her words touched me deeply. For indeed, I often feel kinship with heroic sisters of myth and history. With Sleeping Beauty, who finally awakened from her adolescent sleep to flower as a woman in response to love. With maidenly Psyche who lost her beloved mate when she lit the lamp of consciousness, and through her labors of growth was reunited with him on a higher level of Divine union.[2] With heroic Eowyn who courageously drew her sword against the lord of darkness, and her cheeks wet with a woman's tears, slew him and won the battle.[3]

When did my transforming journey begin? In earnest, ten years ago, when I stumbled, bleeding and frightened from a twenty-five year marriage. I felt anything but heroic then. In the closing months of that shattering drama, a lifetime of self-doubts reared their ugly heads to confront me.

What about the angry harshness I bemoaned in myself so often? I'd been inwardly rebelling against life for as long as I could remember. And my quick defensiveness when I felt attacked? I deplored my compulsive use of my intuitive gifts to serve my anger. What about my supercilious "Proud Independent Lady" self, and so close beneath her, tearful "Miss Pitiful-Please-Take-Care-Of-Me"?

My paradoxes were so deep, my joys so fleeting, my pain so chronic.

Where had the fullness, the wholeness, the joy of my womanhood gotten lost? I caught shining glimpses of that priceless beauty within me. Oh, I yearned for full reunion as a dying soul for living water. How, where could I find it?

This is the naked tale of my searching and my finding. It is a heroine's journey still in progress . . .

Dear sister, is it perchance your story, too?

Helene K. Joy
P.O. Box 1703
Aptos, California 95001

THEME

How is a woman, when she feels the immense fascination of the power of the spirit stirring in her, to welcome it and yet remain true to her womanhood, or how is she to rediscover her femininity if she has lost it? How is a man to realize the values of the heart without losing the bright sword of his spirit in the fogs of emotion? There are no intellectual answers. Only the images by which we live can bring transformation. The future hangs on this quest for the heart of love by both sexes.

Each of us has a well of images within, which are the saving reality, and whence may be born the individual myth carrying the meaning of a life. . . . It must be born out of the crucible of our own struggles and suffering as we affirm our new freedom without rejecting the perennial truth of the feminine way.[1]

Helen M. Luke

1

Turning My Face Toward The Heights

Everywoman has the leading role in her own unfolding life story . . . there are mythic dimensions in everyone.[1]

Jean Shinoda Bolen

But there are not, there cannot be, any ancient stories which mirror the extraordinarily new and difficult inner path which the daughters of this century must tread.[2]

Helen M. Luke

Etched painfully into my memory is the night I first glimpsed this profound journey before me. That night my husband of twenty-four years put evidence of his love affair where I couldn't possibly miss it. And this was no mere fling, he implied.

"I don't know whether I want you or her for my wife," Len admitted, miserable and guilt-ridden.

Oh my God. Toward morning I finally fell into a fitful, exhausted sleep, hugging my side of the bed. Feeling desperately betrayed and alone, I withdrew my energy as well as my body from Len. No doubt that made my dream—or was it a vision?—possible. In my journal, I wrote it:

"I've awakened with an amazing dream which still holds me in its spell. My feet were dancing, flying up a sunlit mountain path; my heart was exultant and free! Range after range of lofty peaks were visible to me under the heavenly blue sky. I was caught up in the wonder and the beauty of my easy ascent, like a wild bird finally freed from a cage. Suddenly I became aware that I'd left someone behind. I looked back for Len and saw him in a deep shadow down near the base of the mountain. He was shuffling around in circles as though looking for something, muttering to himself, 'I'm the romantic type.' (This was an actual

9

statement he was fond of making.) After only a moment's pause, I resolutely turned my face back toward the heights and continued my exhilarating ascent."

I immediately recognized that the dream-vision was a gift from my higher Self. Would that I might have celebrated the gift of freedom life was offering me and eschewed the hellish suffering of the subsequent months. But I had to live out everything in its season. Only after a period of protracted dying was I ready to receive the gift of new life which the vision portended.

> *And think not you can direct the course of love, for love, if it finds you worthy, directs your course . . . He gathers you . . . threshes you . . . sifts you . . . grinds you . . . kneads you . . . assigns you to his sacred fire. . . . All these things shall love do unto you that you may know the secrets of your heart, and in that knowledge become a fragment of Life's heart.*[3]

2

You Must Walk Out of Hell Alone

> *It is as though he has made a superb flight to the sunlit mountaintop, realized its glory . . . but has been brought back reluctantly to the starting point with the rueful recognition that the steep path leading to the heights must be climbed step by step.*[1]
>
> Roberto Assagioli

I had met Len at the Methodist student fellowship in college. Immediately I picked out this tall engineering student with the intelligent brow as the man I wanted for my husband. At twenty, Len's dark hair was already showing some silver strands. I found him marvelously handsome.

We'd come from remarkably similar homes, and he felt like a safe, familiar place. There was a strong physical attraction between us, and, I was convinced, a deep soul resonance as well. But we were barely out of our teens, and so emotionally needy. We each unconsciously saw in the other the possibility of finding the warm, nurturing parent that neither of our childhood homes had provided. So we married quickly, both continuing our college studies. Naturally, things started going awry from the very beginning. We bound ourselves tightly together attempting to get our acute emotional needs met, giving one another scarcely any freedom in the process. Within our mutual dependency we both struggled for dominance, afraid of being swallowed up by the other.

"You're trying to be the head of the family!" Len indignantly accused me many times. Of course, patriarchal marriage customs of those decades gave him the right to claim that role. I shudder to remember my guilt as I desperately resisted what felt like certain annihilation.

But I was caught! For my determination not to be used by my man ran counter to my deepest instincts as a woman. Nor could I attempt to use him for my ends without deeply violating myself. The feminine instinct "is precisely to *use* nothing, but simply to give and to receive. This is the nature of the earth—to receive the seed and to nourish the roots—to foster growth in the dark so that it may reach up to the light."[2]

I knew I wanted and intended to be a good wife to Len. Not only did I need his love and approval, there was genuine caring between us as well as the fear and resentment of our deeply ambivalent union. We shared many high ideals and common interests including our adventuring spiritual search. And as our three beautiful children came along we shared the satisfactions of conscientious parenthood. Both Len and I matured a lot in the process. But even as the children were a bond between us, they also provided a buffer zone, helping us avoid a direct psychological intimacy.

Reading my journals from the last several years of our marriage painfully reminds me how chronically tense, lonely, and resentful I was. I berated myself a lot for spewing angry frustration into the atmosphere of our home. Sometimes I inwardly recoiled as I heard myself turn into a harsh, haranguing bully. Len coped with life by passively retreating inside himself, cutting off from his feelings and from me. When he turned himself into a zombie like that, my misery was devastatingly total.

Much later I would discover Carl Jung's anima-animus model. Animus is his term for a woman's unconscious masculine side, which, unless it is recognized and positively related to, can take over her life—can possess her—in a cruel, negative way. (Her husband's passivity exacerbates her problem.)

Eighty-five percent of animus possession in women is a disguised appeal for love, although it has the wrong effect since it chases away the thing that is wanted.[3]

Even if I had understood this, I would have been unready to apply it. For right beneath my chronic anger was a raw, gaping wound of the heart that would not, seemingly could not, heal. It felt so very ancient in origin. My female organs were expressing this dis-ease as an eroded, weepy cervix that required continual cauterization.

"Where has my wholeness, my joy in being a woman gotten lost?" I barely had the courage to ask. My bleak wilderness journey was punctuated by occasional shining glimpses of inner feminine beauty. But I despaired of reconnecting with those life-giving springs within.

How lost, how far from home, how parted from
The earth, my sister, O my sisters, we have come.[4]

It was into this hellish milieu that our extraordinary young friend, Michael, brought his healing wisdom. I've never doubted it was a case of "When the student is ready the teacher will appear." When we first met him, little did we dream of the crucial role he'd play in our lives! He was an attractive but restless youth in his early twenties, struggling to overcome a long drug dependency. Still, there was already an air of budding spiritual authority about him. One of our church's ministers took Michael under his wise, caring wing. Then Michael dropped from sight, and when he reappeared—in our twenty-second year of marriage—he made us believers in radical transformation!

He'd completed a master's degree in psychology, had discovered and developed his remarkable intuitive gifts under one of California's foremost sensitives, and had seriously embarked upon a disciplined spiritual path. We asked Michael for some counseling help.

Only in that first session did he suggest Len and I encounter each other. With him observing, we hit each other with pillows to the point of exhaustion.

"I'm tired of a husband who tunes me out!"

"I'm tired of a wife who's angry all the time!"

Then I fell into helpless, bitter weeping, and Len into a progressive, fearful withdrawal which left him expressionless and remote. Michael seemed sobered as he watched our toxic way of relating. For he correctly intuited in both of us, "It's *you* I want."

We admitted that to each other, feeling hopelessly sad about ever finding the nourishing emotional connection we'd yearned for so long.

"When you're able to get honest with each other about your pain and disillusionment from the very beginning of your marriage, you'll end up weeping in one another's arms," he told us prophetically.

Then Michael seemed to shift gears, and he spoke more deliberately, more quietly. Did he not look straight at me? I found myself strangely stirred by his final words:

"You know that in many fairy tales a couple meets and marries in the underworld, in a dark, unconscious 'paradise.' But there comes a time in their development when they have to walk out of hell's darkness. It has to be done alone; it cannot be accomplished together. If each succeeds in that demanding task, there's a chance they can find one another again on a higher level—*if* they so choose."[5]

Michael would serve as my beacon during that lonely journey into the light.

3

"You've Sung Only Part Of Your Song"

There is a Power for good in the Universe available to everyone. . . . We all use the creative power of the Universal Mind every time we use our own mind.[1]
Ernest Holmes

You are the creator the Creator created.[2]
Lisa deLongshamp

What we fail to complete, we repeat.
What we resist, persists.
What we fail to forgive, we relive.

Anonymous

There are people who positively insist on being victims over and over again.[3]
Helen M. Luke

I felt a real urgency to meet with Michael again for I trusted him implicitly. I saw that his remarkable spiritual gifts would allow him to discern deep patterns in me which I'd effectively hidden from myself. And if I were to begin the journey out of hell, I knew I needed his heaven-sent wisdom about how I'd gotten in.

You might ask, "How could she know herself so little?"

I could easily trace the loss of much of myself back to childhood, as can so many of us. "What happened to my childhood? Was I not cheated out of it?" we ask ourselves. And the most sensitive, the most talented children can be the hardest hit.

> . . . the child had an amazing ability to perceive and respond intuitively, that is, unconsciously, to this need of the mother, or of both parents, for him to take on the role that had unconsciously been assigned to him . . . this role secured "love" for the child.
>
> For the majority of sensitive people, the true self remains deeply and thoroughly hidden.[4]

And being a woman had also complicated my problem:

> Women have adapted themselves to the wishes of men and felt as if their adaptation were their true nature.[5]

I could not have articulated all this then. But my lack of joy told me that something very basic was wrong. "I must be horribly caught in some contorted, off-center place," I often anguished. "Otherwise my continual efforts to be a better, happier person would surely have availed."

Yes, indeed. On his next visit, Michael confirmed it. I shall never forget that profound day of discovery—I confronted the fact, for the first time ever, that I was a raging inferno inside. I felt like a maligned, innocent victim of life, furious at those I perceived as my victimizers. First and foremost, God!

Michael sat down opposite me, grew quiet, and gave me a penetrating look.

"Why am I so desperately unhappy?" I begged to know.

"You're holding a grudge against your father-God. You are fighting the masculine, and this drains your energy away from yourself as a woman."

I conceived of myself as an intelligent, educated person of the twentieth century. So it amazed me to hear him explain, "Like the biblical Job, you're seeing God as an archetypal power outside yourself who brings down catastrophe and famine—especially *emotional* malnutrition, like a sudden withdrawal of life sustenance."

He got specific. "This was your experience when your sister was born. And you're angry at your Dad because you were no longer number one with him after that."

That certainly rang true. What child has not confused Daddy with deity? I had been an only child for seven years, and remember feeling utterly bereft when love seemed withdrawn after my sister's birth. I had adored my Dad; he had the capacity to express feelings which my mother seemed to have buried. This event left a deep psychic scar, and soon after Carrie's birth I developed asthma and hayfever due to emotional congestion. The skin outbreaks I'd had since infancy also greatly worsened. My rage at my Daddy and my health problems had moved with me right into adulthood.

Now Michael bore in. "But you see, *you* triggered that programming! It's an affect pattern you brought in from previous lifetimes! In many past lives you've gone through a loss of prestige, a removal of status. This time it happened at the early age of seven."

He was firmly laying responsibility for my unhappy life right at my own feet. Embittered toward the masculine—which I'd experienced as rejecting and hurtful—and cut off from the nourishing feminine, I had built for myself an experience of hell on earth.

> *Thus, as in many women of the finest quality, the whole of her feminine unconscious turned negative.*[6]

Michael seemed to know that I'd not be shocked by his reference to reincarnation. Several years before, an esteemed older friend—a Methodist like myself—had introduced me to it.

"This teaching cannot be written off by those seeking truth with sincerity," she'd told me. "Three-fourths of the world's people belong to religious traditions that teach reincarnation. It was a part of early Christianity until the third century when the church fathers deleted it because it diminished the power of the priesthood. But there are still vestigial references to it in our New Testament for those who have eyes to see them."

Strange as that sounded at first, I'd felt it important to look into the teaching.[7] For, as I had held each of my beautiful babies in my arms, I'd deeply pondered the meaning of life and love, things cosmic. Gradually I'd concluded, "This offers an explanation for things I've never understood. My babies were all born bright, healthy, beautiful. But some children seem to come in with two strikes against them. Is the Creator not fair? Is the Universe not friendly? Or does each soul draw to itself the things it needs to experience on the earth in order to grow?" So I was open to the powerful confrontation Michael was dealing me.

He went on, "When your sister was born you came down on yourself. For when a sudden outside event knocks you down a few notches, there's a tape loop in your consciousness that engages. You not only rage against that event *and* against God, but on another level you say, 'This is what I deserve.'"

I flashed on my guilty words to a friend during a painful crisis with Len, "I'm sure this is what I deserve."

"You see," Michael explained, "we all draw to ourselves the life experiences we need to self-correct. But you're perceiving them as punishment instead of just cause-effect. As long as you're living under the concept of sin and guilt, those learning experiences become toxic."

This all rang true. No wonder my sister's birth was so traumatic for me! I'd interpreted it as punishment for not being good, for not being lovable. And my destructive past-life patterns were part and parcel of countless generations' ignorant collective beliefs. I'd reinforced those, this time around, by attracting to myself a Daddy who frequently hid his fears behind long scoldings and moralizing. My spirit often felt horribly crushed under the weight of his dark, judgmental side unmitigated by a Mother's warm, accepting nurturing.

Now I understood the ancient-feeling wound in my heart which seemed to defy healing. Oh God, how ancient! But now Michael offered hope:

"This block will start to clear up when you forgive yourself. But you're going to have to peel off one layer at a time. It's a *big* job!" He spoke truly. At this writing, a decade later, am I finally nearing the core? *I love, I forgive, I release every part of myself to the wholeness that is my birthright.*

Michael sensed my willingness to hear on. I was amazed at my own determination to face anything in order to get free. That, of course, is the positive role of suffering in our lives.

"You're afraid of your own beauty. This comes from those lives where you had prestige, noble rank. You were often beautiful and got caught up in your own glamour which blinded you to the higher light, preventing your development. In order to self-correct you chose times in history in which the rug would be pulled out from under you by insurrection or rebellion—another pattern you've run over and over again." Now he spoke with obvious compassion. "Someday you're going to weep for the pain you've caused yourself." Hot tears started to scald behind my eyes.

"So," he continued, "it's hard for you to accept even your inner beauty now, and this cuts you off from your soul level." No wonder I was grieving for something precious I knew I'd lost! "You need to learn to weep for yourself, for putting your beauty in the closet. Not just your physical beauty but your emotional beauty as well. Tears are your best way of transforming yourself, because then your energies can manifest emotionally through your heart." I recalled how crying was frowned upon by my parents. I had choked back and choked back, trying to be their brave little girl. Now I would have to give myself permission to release that dammed up flow of healing waters.

Michael paused intently as though looking deeper. Then, finally, some good news. "Your heart is incredibly beautiful; your heart center has flames all around it. You've had lives, too, of realizing a lot of the devotional, the higher, impersonal love energies, lives of service . . . " I was deeply moved for I sensed the truth of which he spoke. "You're a deep song," he said more softly. "You've got it learned on one scale, but there's a whole counter movement, a deeper part of your song that you haven't sung." Oh, how I yearned to sing my *whole* song!

Now Michael summed up, "You are beginning to flower. I suggest you work with the book: *Getting Clear: Body Work for Women*.[8] You need to get more into your own woman, to get a sense of yourself *apart* from men before you can come into a better relationship *with* men. Get a sense of self apart from your relationship with your husband, your father, sons—or an alternately wrathful/loving God you've perceived as outside yourself. You're drawn to men because you think that's where the resolution to your pain lies, but your unfulfilled needs will be met as you learn to *give to yourself* as a person and as a woman. Get into some women's groups," he concluded, "and find yourself a female therapist who has it together as a woman."

After he finished, I sat silent in reverent appreciation. Everything he said had clicked. He'd unveiled a vast panorama before my astonished eyes, and I knew that for many difficult years, perhaps lifetimes, I'd groped for these freeing revelations. For a fleeting moment I wondered if Michael were not the archangel visiting me in earthly disguise. For he had delivered a letter from my God-Self, and the keys to hell's exit were in my trembling hand.

17

4

Sleeping Beauty Rubs Her Eyes

Like the butterfly, I find
I can no longer stay behind
Self-made walls of protection.
I struggle to be free,
Breaking the bonds of what was
*   me*
To soar in a new dimension.[1]

Jean Beggs

I could take only slow, small steps toward freedom. Hell had been my abiding place so very, very long.

But my resolve was strong! I began working with the bodywork book Michael suggested. Then I joined a Jungian study group for women and discovered the profound beauty of Irene de Castillejo's classic, *Knowing Woman.*[2] As whole new levels of feminine awareness came my way I was at once nourished and terrified by their implications for my life.

Some truths which I could scarcely grasp with my mind nevertheless sent shivers of recognition up my spine:

> *Women are throwing over their sense of cosmic awareness and the connection of all growing things in order to adopt men's values in their stead. That only serves to upset the necessary balance between the opposite poles. It is now imperative for men and women alike to stretch from pole to pole in order to achieve the paradox of holding both attitudes at once.*[3]

In spite of my enlarging vision, I found I was still unable to consider a future without Len at my side. "Perhaps we can walk out of hell by each taking more growing space within our marriage," I cautiously hoped. "Surely we'll not have to relinquish one another completely."

But the continuing pain of our relationship motivated my decision to begin a master's degree in counseling psychology. This study would be a great stabilizer during the traumatic period ahead.

However, as Michael had pointed out, my greatest need was to get in touch with my feelings, with my healing tears, with the suppressed beauty of my woman's heart and soul.

One night I poured out this tender letter to myself in my journal:

"Dear Virginia, (my name at that time)

I see you rubbing your eyes after a long, unconscious sleep, ready to come alive, awake, aware—ready to discover your own truth and live from your own feminine center.

During this time of sleepwalking you have suffered a lot. I am so sorry. You bumped into things and persons, and were knocked down by other sleepwalkers like yourself. Sometimes you cried from the bruising, but more often you held in the pain and your body wept for you.

Sometimes you grieved for the hurt you caused others from your half-conscious state. More of that recently. But mostly, it was for yourself.

Now I see you awakening, daring to look at parts of yourself that need transforming. Last night you caught a glimpse of your negative, sword-wielding animus, and wept for the pain it has caused Len and the kids. You also recognized Len's anima,[4] and how the two continually, destructively spar.

You're shaken by Michael's words about being afraid of your own beauty. I feel you running to make up for lost time, scared that before you can accept your physical and emotional beauty you'll already be old and wrinkly! May I remind you of the beauty of Edith S. at age sixty?

You're awakening to your fear of vulnerability and tenderness. 'Good Mornin', Pain,' is your song of awakening . . . But, dear lady, I know that joy is *somewhere* on your horizon!"

I learned to sing this wonderful song with my guitar. It became my theme song, surely a part of the "deeper song" I was just beginning to sing.

Good Mornin', Pain

Good Mornin', Pain.
I never thought I'd welcome you again.
I never thought I'd long for you and search
    for you in vain;
But when you went away I walked a desert
    with no rain.
And I'm so glad to have you back again.
Good Mornin', Pain.

Good mornin', Tears.
I never thought I'd long for you to rise.
I never thought I'd miss your misery
    blurrin' in my eyes;
But when you ceased to flow, the springs
    of joy also went dry.
And I'm so glad to hang my head and cry.
Good Mornin', Tears.

Good mornin', Love.
I had to learn you never come alone.
And when I shut out hurtin', something in
    me turns to stone.
To be in touch with tenderness, I'd bare my
    blood and bone.
And I'm so glad to have you back again.
Good mornin', Pain. Good mornin', Joy.
Good mornin', Love![5]

5

"She's A Nutcracker"

Until she loves herself, her loving will be manipulative, dependent, and destructive of the freedom of others since it will not spring from an active, alive, and potent attitude toward the self and the world.[1]
Erich Fromm

I was introduced to princess Psyche in my Jungian group. She is the heroine of the ancient tale, "Eros and Psyche" (or Cupid or Amor and Psyche), a story containing a symbolic road map of maturing womanhood, of feminine "individuation."[2]

Psyche's first difficult, developmental task is to sort a huge pile of mixed seeds. Symbolically, it is every woman's task on her way to wholeness.

> . . . the sorting of the seeds—the immensely painful task of discrimination, of complete honesty, as far as she was capable of it about the thoughts, feelings, and actions of her life. It is the first necessity of the way to consciousness for women.[3]
>
> Sorting the seeds would require an enormous amount of self-discipline . . . and would be the woman's heroic deed.[4]

I had made a commitment to myself to become conscious. Now it seemed life was asking, "Do you really mean business?"

One day I found a note atop my teen-aged son's dresser. Although he'd written it to himself, journal-style, he must have known I'd find it there eventually.

"She's a nutcracker!" Clark began, and continued an eloquent complaint against "her" emasculating harshness. I gasped in hurt surprise, for I was sure he was speaking of me. We'd been having some painful conflict though I really couldn't put my finger on what it was about. I'd often been amazed at Clark's sensitivity and wisdom. Now I shuddered to realize that, for some reason seemingly beyond my control, both my husband and my fine, strong, athletic son perceived me as castrating!

"If this is true," I finally found the grace to say, "I've got to make it fully conscious."

Out in our garage therapy room I took my courage in hand and sketched a life-sized, nude male figure on newsprint. With deliberation I picked up a plastic sword and began slicing and slashing at it while reciting obscenities in my witchiest voice. Soon I was horrified to feel a bitter river of fury spontaneously pour out of my gut. At the end, I heard myself angrily sobbing,

"I HATE WEAK MEN!"

"What is a 'strong man'?" I had desperately asked John Sanford after hearing him use the term at a Jungian lecture years before.

"A strong man is one who can stand up to a woman's animus and not be thrown by it. A woman with a powerful animus needs a strong man to help back it down so she can get in touch with her feelings, with her capacity for relatedness. But a strong man won't marry that kind of woman. He'll choose a different sort. A weak man may marry her because he needs her strength. *But he*

21

does her no good. So she gets angrier and angrier."[5]

Now I collapsed miserably into the pillows. My high goal of becoming conscious slipped far into the background. I would have to sort out those learnings another day, for I was overwhelmed by the bitter feeling that life had cheated me. I hated it.

6

"Mom, You Passed The Baton"

The negative role of bitch is almost built into woman's role and it surfaces at the heart of the duality of marriage if this is the only place where she has a chance to exercise power.[1]

Elizabeth Janeway

... no human being escapes the condition of being influenced by the parents' unconscious. ... The only way, I think, is to take responsibility for what one is, and to make an enormous effort to interrupt the curse or the chain which goes on from one generation to another.[2]

Marie-Louise von Franz

A few weeks after I found Clark's note, Len invited Clark to go with him to a primal-scream workshop. There, both men gave full vent to their anger. Len bitterly scolded his mother for letting him down as a child, and Clark yelled and pounded his rage at me.

The therapist listened with interest to father and son. "How alike the mothers are! Len, you married a woman like your mother."

Small wonder she and I had felt instant, mutual dislike and distrust upon meeting! Much effort through the years on the part of both of us finally enabled us to show hospitality during the infrequent visits.

I was turned off by her cringing fear of life and her emotional coldness. I resented her possessiveness, her over-control and obvious emasculation of her men. (And, admittedly, I was jealous of Len's still strong attachment to her.) She mirrored to me my own worst side! Len had fallen from the frying pan into the fire, still trying to get the same kind of frustrated, wounded woman to love him.

(Only later I realized that Len could not adequately help our son win his freedom—his masculine authority—from the archetypal "terrible mother." For Len was still caught in his own negative mother complex; he'd not yet won his own sword.)

My mother was emotionally similar to Len's, of course. She repressed her feelings and tended to play the martyr. By her own admission she "managed" her younger husband and daughters. Controlling was safer than open-hearted vulnerability.

Counselors of several years gave clues to our predicament: "Both you and Len were raised by frightened people . . . afraid of their feelings . . . hiding behind puritanical moralisms . . . too insecure to realize their full potential."

Len and I grew concerned for our growing children as we saw patterns repeating with the generations. So we conscientiously began a weekly "family meeting" where feelings could be shared and problems resolved. We all learned good communication skills together: how to give "I messages," how to do reflective listening, how to find creative solutions. Our children recall those sessions with great appreciation, still drawing from those skills in their young adult lives.

Len and I took separate journeys to another city for two-week primal therapy intensives—a good start toward peeling off layers of "pure primal rage" Michael had seen locked up inside us both. We brought the modest fruits of this inner work to the family meetings.

On my next birthday—my fortieth—Clark took me aside to give me a heart-warming gift. "Mom, let this little present always remind you that you are loved and you are forgiven. I see now that you simply passed to me the baton given you by your parents and their's before them."

When this beautiful son left for college two years later, I fell into several days of deep travail. In spite of his forgiveness, I was unable to forgive myself for bruising his tender, emerging manhood.

That burden lifted oh-so-slowly over the next several years, and only as I finally learned to love and forgive myself.

7

"I Open My Hand And Let You Go"

Every unshed tear is a prism through which life's hurts are distorted.

Unknown

We all sorely missed Clark's sincere and loving presence. None had realized how important he was to each person in our family.

Our lovely sixteen-year-old daughter, Lynn, hurled a silent, desperate cry after her departing brother: "Don't go away and leave me to face them alone!"

And shy, sensitive, twelve-year-old Rolf spent even more time behind the closed door of his room.

"Our home is such a wasteland," I anguished, uncomprehending. "Len and I intend so well and try so hard."

Our year of family meetings had given the children a positive forum for their feelings, but had scarcely touched the deep, unconscious conflict between Len and me. In hindsight, I see how it poisoned everyone in our home.

I awoke one morning badly shaken by a dream. In my journal, I wrote it: "I watched a man and woman stab each other to death. She fell first, but grimaced and gasped as he bent down and kept stabbing her. Then it seemed that I was the woman, and he, 'my man.' Soon he fell beside me, mortally wounded. As we died, we fervently kissed; we loved each other—and we destroyed each other."

Again I sought help for the hurting inside me, this time from a woman family therapist. She suggested her male co-therapist sit in, and his presence proved strategic. He role-played Len, and spotted my shrewish double messages. In essence, they were, "Grow up and be a strong man for me . . . . But don't get strong enough to leave me."

"Bring your husband and children," they insisted soberly. "We need to work with you as a family unit."

Len and Lynn consented reluctantly only after seeing my desperation. And Clark agreed to catch a bus home from college. Rolf would have none of it.

"This is crazy," I thought during the first session. "The therapists are talking to Clark and Lynn like they are the parents and Len and I the children." Our children's perceptions were impressive, for sure.

24

Lynn: "Mom has a place inside her where she feels, 'Everything would be all right if I had a big, strong Daddy to put his arms around me and take care of me.' Dad seemed to be that for awhile, but he fell down on the job because he has a little boy inside him looking for a Mama. Mom became disappointed and angry."

Clark: "Mom, you're trying to change Dad from a bad father into a good father . . . Dad, you're saying to Mom, 'Mama, I'm hurt; love me, accept me.' "

The therapists responded, "Right on, both of you!, Clark, avoid using your talents to play peacemaker between them. Lynn, don't 'white knight' your Mom when you feel she's under attack from your Dad." They continued, "Virginia seems unable to hear the double messages she's giving Len . . . And Len studies Virginia and then bases his behavior on what response he'll get from her rather than whether he feels *for himself* to be aggressive or passive or sexual . . ."

Now the therapist looked at Len. "Len, why don't you just come on straight instead of crooked?"

"I have painful memories about being rejected."

"There's an awful lot of both of you getting lost in this relationship."

The next morning I arose at dawn and lit the candles under Christ's picture. I put the clarity of that blessed hour into my journal:

"I clearly see I'm bound into this mutual clutching relationship by fear, fear that Len will slip through my fingers and have an affair or worse. This would throw me into the worst of my primal pain: loss of Daddy, Daddy-rejection. But I've known for a long time that someday I'd have to face this agony, just as Len faced his when I had my affair with F.P.

Len, I open my hand and let you go. I loose you and let you go free.

God, I'm scared. How come I also feel such great peace?"

8

The Other Man

We would call it an anima-animus quarrel; the sword crossing of animus and anima . . . consists in a most horrible way of hurting each other in the most vulnerable spots. Just where the man has the most uncertain, delicate feelings, the woman places the thorn of her animus; and where the woman wants to be understood or accepted, the man comes out with some anima poison.[1]*

Marie-Louise von Franz

I stepped into the crucible of the refining fire at exactly the point I dreaded. My up-and-downhill efforts to emotionally release Len left him floundering, and a succession of his female counseling clients caught his romantic projections. Each time I died a little. My journal filled with prayer exercises for letting him go as I desperately affirmed my own strength and beauty without much conviction. When my anger inevitably erupted, I flung at him psychological jargon like "transference" and "counter transference," wanting to draw blood. Much later, Len admitted about one of the women, "I wanted to hurt you—to get even."

"When you both stop denying you're at war," Michael once told us, "there's a chance to clear out your rage and find peace."

I have no doubt that my affair four years previously had been part of that bitter, unacknowledged war. It was also a great deal more than that—an agonized cry for help.

In hindsight I can see it all quite clearly. A few months before I began the affair, I half-consciously sensed my ripeness for "disaster." Infidelity was not acceptable in my value system. So I urgently asked Len to go with me to a marriage enrichment workshop, hoping to breathe some new life into our unnourishing relationship. The workshop I proposed coincided with our nineteenth wedding anniversary so he agreed. Len was pleased with the results since it got us communicating, at least superficially, about more variety in our sex life. But it did not even touch the deep cry of my heart, and I couldn't articulate what that desperate need was. The therapist told Len in parting, "Do something *everyday* to help Virginia feel like a woman."

By spring my desperation had increased with Len's decision to leave engineering and become a counselor-minister in an independent church we'd helped form. I was terribly shaken. I resented the inevitable loss of the ample income we'd come to enjoy. But most of all, even though I had seen Len's natural skills as a counselor, I was well aware of his lack of professional training and emotional preparation for working with female clients. I saw terrifying handwriting on the wall—the wall we'd been unable to breach between us.

I had always been able to express my anger more easily than I could reveal the naked depths of my terror. Now I found myself compulsively lashing out at Len with scalding, punishing criticism instead of supporting him in his vocational change. Intuitively I knew where to aim my angry darts to hurt him the most. In my better moments I cringed as I owned my devastating capacity to wipe him out.

F.P. was a leader in our community whom I'd known for several years. He'd seen me at my charismatic best, leading groups with sensitivity and an ability to inspire. I was aware of his admiration for he'd spoken of it to others, and it pleased me. I found him very attractive: he was a profoundly intense man, strong of feeling and spiritual sensitivity, with a large, broad-shouldered physique. But the ultimate pull: he was lonely, needy.

We linked up powerfully on a heart level one day in his office as we talked over the meeting we'd co-chaired. His unspoken sadness moved me, and as I rose to leave I spontaneously opened my arms to hug him. How can I describe the fiery power of that next moment? Within his suddenly passionate embrace I gasped with the exquisite agony of a burning explosion in my chest. I didn't comprehend till later; it was the "piercing of the heart." My long-standing armor thus penetrated, I was literally never to be the same again. Trembling from the intensity of love I felt for him, I tore myself from his kisses and drove home reeling. Len said wonderingly that night, "I've never felt so much love flow from you before." And I discovered I was giving my children large, healing doses of tenderness.

For several months I half-consciously weighed my fear of an affair with F.P. against my desire. I dared speak of it to no one. Perhaps I was testing to see if Len could now evoke that powerful response in me. It didn't happen. But the merest recall of that day in F.P.'s office and I'd be melting, flowing, enlivened again. Though I feared I might die of the consequences of giving in to my desire, I finally realized that I would most certainly die if I didn't. As a deliberate, conscious act, I called F.P. to tell him of my powerful experience in his arms, and soon we were living out our wildest fantasies.

The effects on me were dramatic. Close friends puzzled: "You're like a different person! You're so much softer . . . . I've never seen you wear pink before; it's lovely on you." How I longed to tell them!

For four months I was awash with incredible joy. F.P. was also sparkling, bringing obvious new creativity to his demanding job. But when he was offered a promotion and transfer to another city, we agreed that he should take it. We feared discovery; but, more than that we feared the very intensity of our relationship as a potential threat to our respective families.

But it was a decision of the head, not the heart. When he left, the fresh singing springs of my tender, passionate love suddenly ran dry. The new life I'd come to depend upon felt cruelly aborted. I was devastated.

"It was another man who made me feel like a woman," I blurted out guiltily to the marriage-enrichment therapist. "I loved him so much I would have died for him. I've never felt that way about a man before."

She was very wise. "This man gave you some openings you were ready for which Len couldn't give you. You are really beginning to flower as a woman. I see no need for you to tell Len about your affair. But perhaps you can now start to bring the fruits of your opened heart to your marriage. Let's hope Len can now meet you in that place of deeper, fuller intimacy."

"That's what I want," I told her. "Len has always been the man for whom I wanted to be a woman."

Alas, I could not bridge the wide chasm of fear and rage between us. "Have we already hurt each other too much?" I despaired. So my heart's juices, requiring an outlet, flowed along my strong psychic connection to F.P. It took two years for that to dry up.

Len sensed that my emotional energy had gone elsewhere. But he was too scared to confront me, and I was too scared to tell him. So we kept hanging on and bleeding.

A horrible year went by before I knew I couldn't stand that dishonesty another day. Terrified, I nevertheless felt compelled to risk blowing apart our crippled marriage by telling him the truth. I also wanted to shake him up—painfully. I loved him and I hated him.

I asked a psychiatrist-friend to help me break the news. But I soon regretted that, for I shrunk up like a guilty child as I heard him patiently explain to Len how my affair was due to early father deprivation and the resulting arrested emotional development. I recognized that what he said was true as far as it went. Oh, how I later kicked myself for lacking the self-esteem to cry out thus in my own defense:

"But there's more! There's a precious new woman inside me struggling to live. Help her, dammit! Where the hell have you been while she's needed you to love her?"

(Two years later I would weep with gratitude to hear Michael confront Len: "Where's your *passion,* your *desire,* your *MAN?* It's those she wants!")

Len was crushed at the news of my affair, then enraged. He broke through to long-buried feelings, and went to the seashore to weep and to curse me for several terrible hours. The wife-mother he'd tried for twenty years to get love from "betrayed me and gave it to another."

Within a few days he offered me his forgiveness. But he continued to pour a silent, poisonous condemnation over me in spite of his best intentions. I am sad to report that since I felt so guilty, I accepted it. "You're nothing but a damn baby!" he blurted out one day, and I felt it go right to my core. He began looking at other women with an affair in mind. Now my tender, insecure feminine growth felt crushed beyond repair.

But the depth of my misery moved Len, and the natural compassion of his basically loving heart flowed to me in shared healing moments. "I love you so much," he wept one day as he laid his hands tenderly on my head in prayer. "If another man can make you happy, I gladly release you to him."

We were tragically caught in a dark web of loving and hating.

9

"Kids, I've Had An Affair"

Love awakens in her . . . the ice round her heart is melted.[1]

Helen M. Luke

Feminine individuation and the spiritual development of the feminine . . . are always effected through love.[2]

Erich Neumann

Three years later I was still feeling unresolved about my affair. Since I had violated my own moral code, I bought heavily into Len's continuing condemnation and punished myself. However, intellectually I was starting to make some sense of it all even while wearing sack cloth and ashes.

Unresolved as I was, I needed to tell Clark and Lynn about it. For it was on the eve of our first family therapy session, and I chose to place my desperate need for healing above my pride. We could not get help without complete honesty; I knew that. And I wanted them to hear about it from me, not Len.

But I felt hesitant, humiliated as I looked at this beautiful son and daughter before me. They had no idea what to expect. Len was also present, obviously ill at ease. The atmosphere was tense.

I took a deep breath to summon my courage and dropped my eyes to the book in my hand. "This is a case history," I told them, "but it could be my story, slightly exaggerated." Then I read aloud:

> *Ellen was raised in a strict religious household; both her church and her parents prescribed a rigid following of a Law. Angry thoughts, disobedient impulses, and especially sexual-erotic feelings toward anyone except a husband were strictly of the devil . . . Insecure, afraid of her own impulses, childlike in her adaptation to life, Ellen married a man who himself reflected all these rigid attitudes, and repressed everything within her which would have led to disobedience. But in time the string ran out on this way of life. Her dark side erupted in a violent and uncontrollable anger directed at her husband. Terrified, Ellen sought help as a flood of repressed, forbidden feelings swept over her.*
>
> *Many months after the first eruption of the unconscious into consciousness, Ellen fell violently in love with another man . . . For the first time in her life she experienced powerful erotic feelings, which led her into an affair with this man which she originally experienced as sublime and beautiful. For the time being guilt was ignored in the beauty of the springlike feelings she was experiencing. Later . . . she realized that she had not loved him as a person, because she had not known him as a person, but had simply experienced for the first time the depth of her own eros.*
>
> *. . . her first impulse was to succumb to the judg-*

30

*mental voices within her. . . . But she was able to see
that her brief love affair was a part of the total meaning of her life . . . her feelings themselves, of eros and
tenderness, were enormously important. Because these
feelings were the motive for her involvement with this
man, she was able to integrate her experience. Had
she set out deliberately to "flout the law"—had this
been her primary motive and not love—the experience
would have been much more difficult to resolve, for
the motivation would then have come from the ego,
and not from her own inner center. Paradoxically,
while she returned to her family, she nevertheless had
to have an experience such as this in order to find the
depths of herself. . . . And it was necessary for her to
disobey the Law and allow herself to be guilty in order
to move into consciousness of herself and a higher
ethic of creativity.*[3]

Encouraged by the serious, polite attention of my loving children, I then went on to tell them about my relationship with F.P.
Though I hardly expected them to understand the subtle psychological nuances of my need to discover my own feminine passion
and tenderness, I needed to give them a thoughtful explanation
for breaking my marriage vows. I so wanted their acceptance!

Clark seemed to take the news quite in stride. But Lynn was
thrown for several days, for she had been feeling a lot of rebellion
toward her parents' "old fashioned morals" and this was unexpected data to assimilate. However, I felt judgment from neither.
I was grateful and relieved that I'd taken the risk of exposing this
hidden side of myself to them.

10

Ripe For Resolution

*But make not a bond of love. . . . The oak tree and
the cypress grow not in each other's shadow.*[1]

Kahlil Gilbran

"I hope you're not planning to leave me," Len said unexpectedly
in our twenty-third year of marriage. "I'm on the verge of a big
breakthrough." I looked at my still-handsome, prematurely gray

husband with surprise, but said nothing. A few months later he remarked, "I'm sorry you're going to leave me when I'm changing so much."

Again I was puzzled. "Does he know something I don't? I've said nothing about leaving." Only in retrospect could I see that I was withdrawing energy from my unfulfilling marriage and redirecting it toward personal growth. Indeed, there were powerful new forces stirring deep within me; Len, ever attuned to anything which threatened his security, was picking up on them. But I was not as strong and independent as I must have seemed. I still desperately wanted him to love and shelter me.

Although we were both making positive changes in our lives, we couldn't envision a future without the indispensable presence of the other. In spite of all the ways we'd hurt each other, the thought of losing our life partner brought wrenching sadness and fright.

Michael strongly recommended more psychotherapy for both of us, this time with a bodywork emphasis, so we began driving some distance each week to work with experienced therapists he knew. Progress was slow but substantial.

Len was stretching and changing, too. Michael compared him to the "Hanged Man" of the Tarot—helplessly dangling upside down while all the attitudes he'd built his life upon now spilled forth irretrievably from his opened-up head.

Our relationship was in an unnerving state of flux, reflecting all the ups and downs of our personal changes. Our compulsive, bitter warfare seemed to surface less often now, but when it did it was all the more painful because of our increasing consciousness. And there were shining, shared moments of healing love.

"You two have a bond, a union that you enacted symbolically on the physical plane by marrying and having children," Michael explained to me once. "But your union with Len goes much deeper on inner planes." My heart confirmed it. Surely it helped explain our tenacity in the face of such destructive obstacles.

But my dream journal now portended a major change. "I'm carrying a bright, beautiful four-month-old baby girl on my left arm," I recorded. "She's so precious to me, I take her everywhere, even to my classes at the university. I have to consider her well-being ahead of even my relationship to Len. She feels like the top priority of my life."

We'd been out of touch with Michael for almost a year when he next came to visit. As soon as he stepped in our front door he sensed the rising pitch of our drama.

"Wow! You're both ripe. Both starting to go through some heavy transformation, including your relationship. I'm sensing a final stage and then a real breakthrough, probably by summer. A resolution is *finally* coming."

What form would it take? I dared not ask. I hardly dared hope.

11

Woman's Mysteries

Each soul enters with a mission . . .[1]

Edgar Cayce

Anybody who doesn't do what they're supposed to in this life has terrible bad luck.[2]

Native American shaman, Rolling Thunder

Before Michael left the next day, I found the courage to edge up to the subject of what lay ahead. I requested some time alone with him.

"Can you give me more detail about the future?" I asked tremulously.

"Yes I can," he said with unmistakable authority. "I see you leading women's groups in a year or two, sharing the levels of personal discovery you're working on now. You are really flowering, involved in one huge change. You'll be sharing a lot of what you're learning with your sisters as a way of making it more your own." Then he paused for emphasis. *"Your life work, your part of the healing Christ flow, is to work with women for at least the next decade."*

He continued, "You'll move out of working with Len; you have your own thing to give." With a rush of excitement my intuition confirmed this, my own life task. But then my stomach suddenly lurched as frightening implications hit me. Though I'd objected to Len's vocational change, it had become meaningful to me as I'd joined him in it. I'd also become ordained as a minister-counselor, and shared the partnership of leading our growth groups. I knew this work was vital to our relationship; sometimes it seemed all that held it together. Oh dear God . . . who would share Len's work if not I? I dared not ask. Nor did Michael volunteer.

He spoke on. "There's a beautiful rainbow over your left shoul-

33

der, the feminine side. I interpret it as a promise that this incredibly long storm of purgation is finally passing, that you'll not have to work through these heavy things ever again." I flashed on my dream about the precious baby girl I carried on my left arm. Yes, it all added up. I felt sure that many lifetimes of suffering were finally being laid to rest. I sighed deeply with relief and gratitude.

And there was much more rich understanding to come from that hour. Michael now introduced me to a profound subject, the "mother-daughter mysteries."

Our daughter, Lynn, had worked hard to graduate early from high school. She was not only eager to try her wings; unconsciously, I'm sure she wanted to escape the pain of a home in crisis. She'd joined a new group of young friends on the east coast where she was looking for her first job.

"You and Lynn are going through a similar process," Michael perceived. "She left the womb of this family even though she is terrified. Her movement is resonating in you, evoking, in part, your own development. She's connected to you very deeply, and I'm aware of her drawing strength from her sense of relationship with you. You're both developing your feminine consciousness, walking hand in hand, but stumbling along. When one starts to pause, the other takes a step . . . A lot of your growth is tied into your daughter's becoming her own woman. It's really the death of a child."

I thought of Lynn with her sweet face and lovely, long brown hair. And I recalled the stubborn strength with which she pursued her goals. "Yes, I see."

She came through beautifully; I was so proud of her. After a few scary weeks she found a clerking job in a large department store, and soon she'd been given the key to the cash registers so she could lock up at night and put the money in the office safe. "I have very authoritative energy, Mom," she reminded me in her exuberant letter. True; we'd often been impressed by that quality in her. I was sure the manager had forgotten she was barely seventeen.

My breakthrough took longer. The "incredibly long storm of purgation" deepened ominously before it finally gave way to the rainbow of the promised new day.

12

Dying To Be Born

*For everything there is a season . . . a time to be born
and a time to die.*

Ecclesiastes III

*When you invoke very powerful energies, you have to
take the consequences.*[1]

Eileen Caddy

Michael was right about a breakthrough in the summer. It
occurred during the days I helped my mother die.

This time I participated in the mother-daughter mysteries as
the daughter. As my mother gradually let go of her earthly life,
I also found grace for relinquishment: of her, Dad, and especially,
a deeper letting go of Len. There in her hospital room, Mother
and I shared a final, profound passage, conscious dying.

Truly, her room became a holy of holies for two days following
her exploratory surgery. (Her tumors proved inoperable.) She was
heavily sedated which put her personality to sleep, but I felt her
higher essence in the room as a loving friend. I felt reassured,
"All is in order." I'd never loved her as deeply, as cleanly, as then.

I brought to her bedside one of my treasured sources of inspiration, the writings of modern mystic, Joel Goldsmith. Several
years earlier I'd discovered his enlightened teaching during a
period of deep spiritual hunger, and a regular study of his mys-
ticism had become an important part of my life, feeding my awakening spirit. Now I partook with great urgency to strengthen both
Mother and me in our life-death transitions.

> *Spiritual progress demands that every form be bro-
> ken, no matter how good it is. If we were willing to
> surrender each day what we had yesterday, we would
> find something better tomorrow, but our very attempts
> to hold on to what we have takes it away from us by
> force . . . Only in what we give up will we ever find
> our Self.*

Surely he was now speaking directly to me:

The [spiritual] student who is at the stage of watching his friends and relatives drop away ... sometimes becomes fearful and begins clutching ... at the wrong thing or wrong person. And why? Because he cannot take aloneness, and if he cannot endure aloneness, he cannot enter into this life. ... We do not always realize that once this transition has been made ... we will be led into the companionship of those of our own spiritual household ... free to make the journeys sometimes necessary to be in their company.

During those long hours of meditative vigil beside my dying mother, I was lifted to a new level of trust in the Divine Plan—whatever it might be—for the next stage of my life. Again Goldsmith spoke to me:

I live by the Spirit of God, not by external things, thoughts or persons. ... Of my own self, I am nothing. ... There is a Spirit within me, a Presence, a Power. I watch how It goes before me, and witness the miracles It performs.[2]

Now I absolutely knew I could depend upon It! My yearning for the freedom to follow that larger Plan was now stronger than my fear of the cost, though little did I dream of the price still to be paid. One by one I laid my loved ones upon the altar of my heart. For what seemed like the millionth time, I said inwardly to Len, "I love you and I let you go." At that moment I was amazed to feel an unfamiliar snapping sensation in my solar plexus, then a strange emptiness followed by a burst of light. Another layer of our clutching, symbiotic connection must have been released! Mother stirred restlessly in her sedated sleep. Was she, at some level, also letting go of Dad?

I called Len that night to report on Mother's condition. He sounded almost panicky. "Call me every day; I don't want to lose touch with you!" I knew then that he'd felt me letting go. I learned later that he initiated a romantic correspondence with a former client that week, perhaps that very day. But he wasn't ready to give me up. So he rented a post office box to keep the love letters secret.

Mother was able to leave the hospital and die in her own bed, as she wanted to, six weeks later. My sister came from Hawaii to care for her; then, a cousin. So Len, Rolf, and I pulled our little sailboat up to our favorite mountain lake and pitched our tent for a short vacation. The beauty there refreshed me as always; yet, I soon intuited something frightening which I couldn't or wouldn't define. Twice I awoke from the same nightmare: Len had left me for another woman. In the middle of one night I awoke to find myself sitting bolt upright, screaming: "MY MOTHER IS DYING AND SOMETHING ELSE IS TERRIBLY WRONG. I DON'T KNOW WHAT IT IS!" Len, lying startled beside me, turned ashen. He knew. He was spending hours in romantic fantasies of Saralynn by this time; he dared only say, "I've been going through some rough things the last month, but I can't share them with you." I was hardly consoled.

We interrupted our camping to attend a workshop in San Francisco and found one of Len's counseling clients there. Len directed his considerable flirtatious charm toward her all weekend, even while wanting me comfortingly by his side. Of course, she loved his attention. I was mute and miserable.

Later I painfully remembered Michael's words, "When your sister was born you made a life statement about yourself: 'I'm second.' " I realized I had to take responsibility for my part in these all-too-familiar triangles, and by the time we got back to camp I was almost a basket case. Belatedly, I confronted Len with my hurt and angry feelings.

He acknowledged sadly, "I'm aware that I pay more attention to other women; I'm dismayed. I am so lonely and hungry for contacts with women, and I feel a great dissatisfaction in our relationship."

"Oh God," I agonized in my journal, "I'm hurting and he's hurting . . . " Then suddenly I felt indignant. "Dammit, I now rescind the life statement I made about being second. I want a love flow with *my* man."

"I want you," I told him with an aching heart. "I want so much to find a more whole kind of love with you."

"I want you, too," he said, "but I'm afraid you'll put down my dependency needs as you've always done before. . . . Will you wait for me?" Acknowledging his pain and confusion, he added, "I'm releasing myself to God's perfect will." I felt touched by his obvious sincerity.

How hard to complete the letting go! As Len pulled the boat from the water for the last time, he felt a sharp sadness. "Somehow I doubt we'll ever be back." Deep inside we both sensed the ending of an era. We hardly dared speak of it. But the grieving had begun.

37

13

Goodbye, Mother

*Woman needs to give. . . . Life pours through her and
she has no choice but to pass it on, or let it stagnate
until it becomes an abcess in her breast.*[1]
>   Irene Claremont de Castillejo

People do the best they can.[2]
>   Ted Lyon

There was simply no time to further process the vacation;
Mother was failing fast. I packed my bags and returned to her
bedside, wanting to be totally present to her and Dad until she
departed the earth.

During the long hours she slept I reflected on what she had
taught me by her living, and now, her dying.

Mom had often quoted Emerson. For instance, she taught us
about life's tradeoffs: "For everything you gain you lose something; for everything you lose you gain . . . "

She wanted us to go beyond her own development in our lives.
"Each generation stands on the shoulders of the one preceding
it," she told us.

I valued her wisdom, her integrity, her commitment to truth.
And now I felt sad that she'd failed to develop so much of her
spiritual sensitivity. Seer Jack Schwarz[3] scolded her about that
once: "People in your church are hungry for a deeper dimension
of understanding which you could teach them. Why aren't you
developing and sharing your intuitive spiritual gifts?"

Her answer surprised me. "Oh dear, I don't want my husband
to think I'm crazy." Though she dominated Dad in many ways,
she always acknowledged with pride his superior brains and education. Obviously his approval was important to her.

Len and I were scarcely engaged when Mom took us aback by
flatly announcing, "There'll be no divorces in *my* family." Might
she also have said, "I'd die before I'd witness such a thing."?

What a blow to Mom's pride to learn she was dying of lung
cancer! "Why, I've never smoked a cigarette in my life!" she complained, uncomprehending.

It was Michael who helped me understand her illness. "She has
a long-standing emotional hurt in her heart center which she's

never released. That stagnant energy has finally turned back upon itself, crystallized and become toxic. That's what cancer is, you know."[4] I was aware of Mom's unresolved childhood hurt over her father's favoritism toward an older, tomboy sister who'd worked with him in the fields. She alluded to it rarely as I grew up, but when she did, I felt the depth of her pain and wanted to weep for her. Tragically, Mom had seemed to unconsciously conclude that to be accepted, a girl must masculinize herself.

Coming from that emotionally injured place, it's no wonder she created for herself a disappointing marriage. Dad was a man of high principles, as well as brilliant and charming, but he was very insecure. His chronic fears were naturally exacerbated by the Depression, for he'd lost one job and feared losing another. I remember how he constantly reached out for Mom's stoic strength. As a little girl I worried a lot and felt disgusted, too, because my Daddy was so scared and my Mama had to give him long cheerful lectures to persuade him he could make it.

But when the powerful hormonal changes of childbearing plunged Mother into unfamiliar vulnerability, it was she who reached out for strength. She felt dreadfully unsupported by Dad during those frightful, lonely hours.

"It hurts to be a woman," Mom told me with bitter disappointment as I grew up.

If she had been able to deal with that hurt, to go through it and come out the other side, she would have found the beauty of her femininity. She would have been a different kind of woman-model for me and my sis. How we needed to see a woman's tenderness, born of the courage to feel her pain and rage, to cry her tears, to release her heart to healing!

The natural joy in being a woman, repressed into the unconscious, drinks the blood, eats the life out of those around such a woman.[5]

What a gift emotional honesty in both our parents would have been! It was a rare commodity in their generation of "good Christian folk." Denial and projection of "unworthy" feelings were more common than not. But how impoverished this left a generation of us children! Because Mom could not cry for herself, she could not let us weep for ourselves, either. "Don't cry; it hurts my ears," she'd frown at her little girls.

BUT WHEN I SHUT OUT HURTING,
SOMETHING IN ME TURNS TO STONE!
TO BE IN TOUCH WITH TENDERNESS,
I'D BARE MY BLOOD AND BONE!
GOOD MORNING, PAIN.
GOOD MORNING, TEARS.
GOOD MORNING, LOVE!

All this came up as I watched my mother die. And I was further confronted by my psychotherapist: "You've lived for your mother; you've never lived for yourself. One of the greatest gifts you could have given her would have been honesty about your real feelings."

My few attempts to do that had produced defensiveness in her. If I'd had the courage to persist, to share with her the fruits of my therapy, would she have had the courage to let them in? How sad I felt pondering these questions at her bedside as she gradually grew comatose, past all chance of communication.

Later I would understand how she also fit the mold of women who grew up at the beginning of this century. Esther Harding, a wise woman of Mother's own generation, enlightened me thus:

> *Only with great difficulty have women extricated themselves from the feminine role which history has provided for them, and learned a new self-respect and independence. . . . But this lesson could only be acquired by keeping feelings strictly under control. All their energies have been engaged in developing the masculine side of their nature, and nothing meantime has been done toward disciplining and developing the feminine instinct which yet remains the most powerful force within them.*[6]

I am grateful for the peace I feel recalling the last few days of Mom's life. The night before my sister, Carrie, returned to Hawaii, we had our last conversation with her. As she lay on the sofa, her daughters drew their chairs close. Our sharing was poignant, sweet.

Carrie and I drew her out, and, enveloped by our love, she eagerly reminisced. Growing up as one of thirteen children on the farm, she'd found her niche as a second mother to her many younger siblings. Though her father had shown favoritism toward the tomboy sister, her mother had appreciated Mom's indispensable help in the house. "Have you forgiven Aunt N. for currying favor with your Dad?" Carrie asked gently. "And your Dad for giving N. more allowance because he said she worked harder?"

"Yes, I feel I have," Mom said with conviction.

"And what unfinished business might you have?" I asked quietly.

"Well, I've not quite finished my grandchildren's quilts," she worried. She was relieved by our suggestion that her church group would gladly show their love for her by finishing them. (And they did.) Then she spoke caringly of her children and her grandchildren; she felt we were all "established" and able to live our lives well without her.

"And have you been able to relinquish Dad?" Carrie asked softly.

"Well, not quite. That's the hardest."

There was a great peace upon the three of us as we tucked her into bed. "You girls make me feel so good," was her way of saying thank you. We had accomplished the three things necessary for a terminally ill person to "die well." We had helped her make existential sense of her life, to tie up loose ends, and we'd given our implied blessing to her leaving us. Mother and daughters had said goodbye.

She appeared to close the shutters of her life after that, and slept a lot as she awaited death. From her final, brief coma, she slipped quietly away.

Dad and I were in no hurry to call the mortician that afternoon. Since she'd requested cremation there was no urgency. Besides, we needed time—time to see that indeed she had gone, that her body was an empty shell, now cooling and discoloring. And time to pray, each in our own way, for her safe passage.

My studies in esoteric religious teachings had convinced me that the newly-dead are closer to the earth vibrations than to the heavenly helpers who come to meet them. Thus, many religions pray for their dead to "boost" them across. I felt some urgency about assisting her full withdrawal of consciousness from her body since it would be cremated the next day. But I didn't know how!

"Lord, I don't know how to pray for the dead," I began with a heavy heart. I waited. Then I found myself singing a flowing, improvised chant with the single, oft-repeated word "Alleluia!"

As I spontaneously lifted my voice in song beside my mother's body, I felt a great surge of spiritual power pour through me. The room seemed to fill with an invisible glory as earth and heaven fused. I lost all sense of time, caught up in the shining wonder of it. The song finally drew to a close as the energy waned, and I knew, without a doubt, that my spiritual midwifery was completed. Then Dad and I peacefully, yet sadly, relinquished her empty frame.

Lonely for her, I raised high my intuitive "antennae" to try to sense her across the veil. For two days I felt absolutely nothing. But the third morning I stepped into her room and she was there! Though not visible to my eyes, she was more present, more alive and more loving than I'd ever experienced her while in the flesh. Her personality barriers to open-hearted loving all seemed to have dissolved. Her clear, warm energy was almost palpable.

I joyously addressed her with my thoughts, "Well, I see you're here today!" I felt her love flowing to me with much the same power and purity as that day in her hospital room when I communed with her higher essence.

With a grateful heart I acknowledged her love. "Yes, I love you too," I mentally told her. "Yes, we do understand each other; yes, we are pals."

My sons, back home, also received a visit from her that day. I was touched to hear about it upon my return, for it more than confirmed my own experience.

The brothers were sharing a relaxed meal when they simultaneously became aware of her presence. Rolf gratefully told me, "Grandma was so peaceful and happy. I've always believed in life after death, but now I know it's true in my gut."

Her message to Clark seemed more specific. "Tell them all, Clark. Tell them *there is no death*." She was adamant; he felt her waiting, then, for his response.

"All right, Grandma," he silently promised. "I'll tell them." Then she went her way in peace.

Truly Mother had died well, which included her convincing assurances that she had really not died at all.

14

The Storm

The best things that ever happened in my life were the windstorms . . . [1]

Elizabeth Kubler-Ross

I am at a loss to describe those next few weeks. Even from the vantage point of this writing I feel overwhelmed by the immensity of the task. For it was just three weeks after I helped my mother die that Len revealed his desire to leave me. How do I speak of death after death after death? I could not possibly except for the resulting birth after birth after birth.

Imagine that you're blown high into the thick of a powerful storm, tossed to and fro among the dark, thundering clouds. You cry out again and again; never have you known loneliness so deep nor terror so total. Soon you realize that to resist this power is to die; the only way to survive is to yield to it. And somehow, you begin to trust. Lightning bolts crash through the howling cacophony, revealing vistas you've never dreamed of on earth or in the heavens. Momentarily you forget your fear and yearn for the tongues of angels to tell what you have seen. Other bolts pass through your own body, and because you resist them not, they electrify you without destroying you.

As the winds abate they gently toss you down upon new, uncharted terrain. Still trembling, you begin to explore this new place. And in time you realize that the storm was your Friend; its name, Love.

15

Discovering Love's Depth

And ever has it been that love knows not its own depth until the hour of separation. [1]

Kahlil Gilbran

"You'll end up weeping in one another's arms," Michael had predicted long before. Finally it came to pass during our last weeks together.

Within days of Mother's death I discovered Len's long-distance romance with Saralynn. He virtually put the evidence under my nose.

"Subconsciously I guess I wanted you to find out," he admitted miserably. "I didn't tell you because I didn't want to burn my bridges with you." He added wretchedly, "I don't know whether I want you or her for my wife." Oh my God.

Now he reluctantly revealed their secret plans to rendezvous somewhere in the midwest a few weeks hence. "I've never even kissed her," he said huskily. "I must see her! I must find out!" Adamant, yet imploring, suddenly full of doubts, he looked gaunt and old. He was scared.

And I was shattered. So great was my trauma that for two weeks I could hardly eat. In those fourteen days I dropped a pound a day. The fact that I'd wanted to be about fifteen pounds slimmer brought little comfort then. For, at some intuitive level I seemed to know that, Saralynn or not, our marriage had sustained its death blow.

I still wanted, needed to deny that. So when a pastor-friend suggested that I might find my marriage to Len stronger on the other side of this drama, I clutched at the hope for awhile. Later I discovered that I simply had no heart to try again. Period.

As we got in touch with the pain of our uncertain future, our hearts opened and softened. Sometimes together, sometimes separately, we remembered tender moments like the sweetness of our kiss at our wedding. Like delightful Christmas mornings with our children. And times when our shared ministry had been fulfilling, bordering on the awesome. Several times we held one another and wept, sharing our feelings more honestly than at any time in our marriage. And our sexual intimacy held new passion, new urgency. During the tender moments following, I'd silently bless Len as I held him in my arms, asking God to guide him wherever his true path led. "I didn't know how much I love him till now," I acknowledged with my broken-open heart.

But most of my weeping was alone. I drove Rolf to his private school in the mountains and I'd often stay for hours, curled up in a clump of redwoods, to weep and to pray. Instinctively, I went back to the womb of mother nature to die and be reborn.

One day I heard my own convulsive sobs and guttural cries filling the hushed, cathedral-like forest. "My God, I sound like a wounded animal," I realized with alarm. When finally spent with exhaustion, I had the feeling I might have turned my lungs inside out. Deep primal layers of hurt and terror were letting go. Had

Michael heard me, he would have encouraged:
"You're hitting paydirt! You're getting your woman back!" Yes,
I was. And the price seemed incredibly high.

At nights I slept poorly. Many times I arose in the pre-dawn
blackness to go out to walk alone. When an occasional car would
slow down beside me, no doubt wondering what a woman alone
was doing on suburban streets at night, I barely registered alarm.
Perhaps I was courting death. But I was doing more than that.
My eyes searched out the stars, and they always reminded me
that I was a part of a large, dependable Universe.

"There's a path ordained for my life, too. I know it is magnificent. I can trust it."

In rhythm with my steps, I'd quietly sing hymns to bolster my
faith. So these walks became meditations in motion. As fall moved
toward winter I still found it necessary to take those long, cold,
lonely walks to sustain my spirit.

Each week I drove to another city to see my bodywork psychotherapist. Prescott was a great blessing during those months and
in the major changes ahead. His caring, yet wise, professional
manner gave me an anchor point of stability in my collapsing
world. I was so full of tears for months that convulsing sobs would
start as soon as he suggested, "Begin deep breathing." In his
wisdom, he never tried to distract me from that weeping, but sat
by supportively watching my frozen past break loose. Perhaps he
wondered, as I did, whether I was not discharging many lifetimes
of grief. I felt like I'd never reach the bottom of that turbulent,
swollen well.

16

"Let This Cup Pass"

*. . . one is like a caterpillar undergoing the process
of transformation into the winged butterfly. The in-
sect must pass through the stage of the chrysalis, a
condition of disintegration and helplessness.*[1]

Roberto Assagioli

I knew there was a deep, transformative process at work in me.
Even in the thick of my protracted weeping, I sensed that it went
far beyond the personality wailings of a fearful, abandoned child-
woman.

"Can the soul also weep?" I wondered. For the tears seemed to water the swelling, bursting seeds of new life stirring within me.

One memorable night during the worst of my dark night of the soul, I slipped from the bed leaving Len heavily asleep. In our therapy room I prostrated myself upon the mattress and cried out with the agony of emotional pain wracking through my exhausted body.

There I drifted into a feeling identification with Jesus—the night he sweat blood in the garden—and I heard a familiar-sounding prayer tear itself from my lips:

"Oh God, I love Len. And I need him; I want to keep him. If it be possible, let this cup pass from me." Only after more deep travailing could I push through my resistance to finishing the prayer. "Nevertheless, not my will but thine be done."

With that came partial peace. Though I saw that my relinquishment was not yet complete, I understood the significance of that anguished hour.

> *In certain moments we cannot tell the difference between transformation and annihilation. For those of us who can face this in ourselves and emerge knowing the greater wholeness, our very presence may help birth the profound transformation that is occurring in our world.*[2]

17

"Become That Powerful In Loving"

> *Usually women in the end get slowly sick of their negative animus. If they don't, they can probably never be cured. But a normal woman usually gets sick of her neurotic side and one day puts an end to it.*[1]

> Marie-Louise von Franz

Benumbed with grief, I hardly noticed that Christmas was approaching. In spite of winter's chill, I kept taking my long, meditative walks just to stay sane. One lonely evening I paused before a neighbor's lighted, outdoor creche.

"Is it really almost Christmas?" I felt like a wounded sleepwalker shocked momentarily awake. I gazed absently at the familiar figures: the holy family, the shepherds, the animals.

Unexpectedly, my whole attention was captured by Joseph, who stood in his usual, humble place behind Mary and the child. "Joseph! It's as though I've never seen you before!" Warm waves of aliveness swept through me as I felt my heart open to him in gratitude. "You were a man so trustworthy, so dependably strong, that God could entrust these precious ones to your protection. Your's was a cosmic task that changed the course of history. You were loving, wise; yes, fearless." (All the qualities *my* man seemed then to lack.) "Never again will I fail to see and honor you, dear brother. I embrace you now as beloved part of me."

Now tingling with excitement and anticipation, I walked on letting more thoughts surface. Suddenly I connected with an awareness of my harsh inner masculine self, so unlike Joseph! How brutally this self often took over my life. What cruel destruction he left in his wake! I stopped abruptly, healthily indignant. Stamping my foot on the sidewalk, I spoke to him with authority as though he were standing right there in front of me: "Never again! As powerfully as you've swung your sword, become that powerful now in loving!"

I was amazed to feel a subtle change take place within me. It was as though my inner furniture were being rearranged. I had begun to take charge! I had been heard! (From this experience evolved an exercise I use in my women's workshops.[2])

Much later I would read:

> *A woman usually lives some time during her life under the domination of . . . the animus. . . . However, once a woman sees the animus, he can no longer be dominant in her psyche. When she knows she has an animus and she relates to him, she is no longer subservient . . .*
>
> *It is one of the great dramas in the interior life of a woman when she challenges the animus' supremacy and says, "I will look at you." . . but in so doing she plunges herself into a loneliness that is nearly unendurable. That is why the stalemate, the domination . . . goes on for so long. A woman knows intuitively that if she breaks up this state of animus possession, it brings the most hellish kind of loneliness.[3]*

I was cutting free from the domination of my inner man and my outer man simultaneously. In the process, my woman was getting free to live. Indeed, I had never known such frightful loneliness. But that difficult Christmas season gave me a profound gift toward my new, more whole and loving life.

18

"Grow or Die"

No real psychological relationship is possible between a dominant and a dependent individual.[1]

Esther Harding

For consciousness, we are apt to pay a Promethean cost.[2]

Robert Johnson

Occasional shining glimpses of freedom encouraged my heart during those weeks of heavy change. I began my story by telling you of the dream I had that cataclysmic night —how my feet were dancing, flying up a sunlit mountain path. What exhilaration to feel kinship with an unfettered bird! But it required my leaving behind someone I loved and depended upon.

Now I rediscovered the ancient tale of feminine individuation, "Eros and Psyche," and identified with the heroine's lonely journey. Early in the story Psyche is told by her husband, Eros, that she must never see his face, must not know his identity or he will leave her forever. He, an Olympian god who has surreptitiously wed this mortal princess, comes to their marriage bed in the dark of night and leaves before every dawn. Jungian interpretations of the tale spoke directly to me:

> *She was imprisoned in darkness, but now the drive toward light and knowledge has become imperious; at the same time she senses that a great menace is gathering over her head . . .* [3];

A great menace, indeed! But in spite of her fears, Psyche finally *must* disobey Eros, and she lights a lamp with which to behold him as he sleeps. (Eros also represents her inner man, her animus, whom she must now recognize and bring into consciousness.)

The knowing Psyche, who sees Eros in the full light . . . is no longer naive and infantile in her attitude toward the masculine . . . She is so changed in her new womanhood that she loses, and indeed must lose, her lover. In this love situation of womanhood growing conscious through encounter, knowledge and suffering and sacrifice are identical . . .
Eros did not want such a Psyche! He threatened her, he implored her to remain in the paradise-darkness, he warned her that she would lose him forever by her act.[4]
. . . he wants his paradise, but no responsibility, no conscious relationship. There is a bit of this in every man.[5]
[But Psyche's] unconscious tendency toward consciousness (here toward consciousness in the love relationship) was stronger than anything else, even than her love for Eros . . . The loss of her lover in this moment is among the deepest truths of this myth; this is the tragic moment in which every feminine psyche enters upon its own destiny.[6]

From my present vantage point, halfway up the whole-ly mountain, I see that Psyche's inner drive toward light and consciousness has been one of the themes of my journey. And not mine alone, but of many women I meet. I'm sad to relate that I've seen very few long-term marriages with vitality. The exceptions are those in which the courageous mates have emotionally released one another (and themselves!) to grow toward their own light wherever that leads. As they've endured the anguish of setting their beloved free, a miracle seems to have occurred: each has gratefully brought that expansion, that new freedom and more conscious capacity for mature loving, back to the marriage union which is then enormously enriched. But there's no guarantee of that at any point. And if one counts on that outcome, one hasn't really let go. I deeply respect these courageous people; I know very few of their ilk.

My mother responded to Jack Schwarz' challenge to light the lamp, "I don't want my husband to think I am crazy." She might also have said, "What you're suggesting is radical; it could break up our marriage."

Which prompts me to acknowledge that my mother's death was strategic in my next steps toward freedom. In fact, within a few months of her transition both my sister and I were painfully tearing ourselves loose from long-term marriages. For us it was now a matter of "Grow or die."

19

"Do I Know This Woman?"

. . . the beginning of independence is often the point where anger and hatred take over and the person is driven to burst the bonds of his former acceptance. He will no longer take what he accepted before. This is often seen by others as evil, which proves that what looks one way can be another. The shadow[1] is truly a liberating force when the person concerned understands something of the great purpose of the negative; and it is important that he understand, especially as few others are likely to.[2]

David Hart

. . . the shadow may reinforce the logos urge toward consciousness.[3]

Frances Wickes

But I run ahead of my story.

Like Psyche, I could gather my courage only by degrees. It took three months of learning to draw strength from within for one day at a time, before I felt strong enough to approach Len about a separation. Even then, my tears brimmed over as I suggested, "You should find an apartment of your own. Then you'll have the freedom to be involved with all the women you want. After a year or so, we can see where we're at with each other."

Len looked startled. But he did spend that afternoon going through the motions of looking at nearby apartments. However, that evening he came home from his weekly session with his psychotherapist to announce, "It's *you* I want!"

I was momentarily stunned, then puzzled by my own reactions. "Why isn't my heart leaping for joy?" I wondered. "After months of waiting to hear those words, of hanging over the precipice?"

Through the weeks Len had been watching my obvious metamorphosis with interest and admiration. This had deepened his own turmoil. My suggestion that he move out brought his crisis to a head.

His therapist had challenged him that night, "Well, Len, decide what the hell you want!"

"So I spent an hour at the marina," he told me, "and I did decide. I want a woman who shares my adventuring spiritual search, a woman who is mentally stimulating, and one to whom I can relate emotionally and sexually. I realized that *you* are the one who fills the bill on all counts."

He continued,"I want to apologize for the way my fear of a deeper intimacy with you caused me to look elsewhere." But then he seemed wistful as he added, "I know I'd really blossom with a non-threatening woman, but I'd probably outgrow her."

"Yah!" I agreed too heartily. "You'd soon find her boring as hell! I know I'm the opposite of non-threatening. I'm creative, I'm talented, I'm a free spirit who has begun to soar!" How good I felt finally acknowledging myself!

"Yes, you are all those things." But his voice was flat and weary. The next day he brought me flowers.

He communicated to Saralynn his decision to stay with me. The plans to tryst with her were cancelled; he burned her letters and asked her to do the same. He sorrowfully acknowledged to her that he'd betrayed a trust as her counselor, and he didn't see how she could help but be hurt and angry, which she indeed was.

More of his chickens came home to roost. His client from the San Francisco workshop also felt betrayed by his failure to follow through after months of seemingly serious flirtation. She had now become Prescott's client, and he suggested she confront Len with her feelings. She did; he was shaken by the encounter.

Though Len had made the choice to focus his energies in our marriage, he now experienced the same difficulty I'd bemoaned after my affair. His emotions ran like wild horses, mainly back to Saralynn-fantasies, even while his will was ordering "Home!"

"I finally understand about you and F.P.," he said uncomfortably.

A new thing now happened in me. My tears abated and I got in touch with a powerful indignation. "He says he wants me. But I feel no love, no warmth, no passion. Again he's asking me to wait for him. After all I've suffered, has anything really changed?"

Now it was Len's turn to feel betrayed. What had happened to his tearful, waiting Virginia? Though her scalding indignation felt familiar, this person confronting him was not the same angry female he'd once known. Her anger was cleaner, more direct, held new authority. She was standing in a more conscious, grounded

place. She was terrifying to him, and strangely exciting to me.
I joined Len in wondering,
"DO I KNOW THIS WOMAN?"

20

"He Sees You As Mama"

*The reason our popular concept of love is so poten-
tially demonic for the woman in this culture is that
it encourages her to surrender her very being to another.*[1]

Penelope Washbourn

*. . . they cannot . . . achieve a conscious relationship
until they know themselves as psychically separate.*[2]

Helen M. Luke

"I'm in great turmoil," I sighed as I unloaded my confusion on
Prescott. "Len says now that if anyone moves out it will have to
be me. I haven't decided. . . "

A few weeks later I reported, "We are still living under the
same roof, trying to take responsibility for our own feelings, and,"
I paused with another anguished sigh, "praying for a miracle."

"You can waste a lot of your life that way! I'd like to see you
get extricated from that symbiotic marriage. I feel like you have
the strength to do it now." No, not quite, Prescott. Our marriage
teetered on.

Len and I were making a last ditch effort to put our lives back
together. We attempted to create closeness by giving one another
sensuous massages, by becoming more playful and romantic.
Those things felt sweet in the moment but left me disturbed and
off-center. My allergies flared up terribly.

"Your new growth is being pushed out of gear by your staying
there," Prescott confirmed one day. "If you need to separate yourself gradually out of your and Len's symbiosis, at least own that
it's your fear that's still holding you there. If you remain honestly
present to your fear, it will pole-vault you into the next level of
growth."

One day I tearfully told Prescott something that was stuck in
my craw. "Three years ago Len got emotionally involved with a
client named Maggie. In my fear of losing him, I gave myself

away to him body and soul. He was ecstatic! At first I felt really loved and cherished, albeit swallowed up. But soon after he felt me totally there for him, he started acting-out with other women even more. I was terribly confused. Angry, too, because I felt he'd tricked me. And some precious, final hope inside me seemed to die."

"Well sure, as long as Len knows you'll be there for him—that the nest is secure—he gets romantically involved elsewhere. He doesn't see you *as a person,* but as a Mama who's an extension of his own needs. You know, like an infant perceives its mother's breast. Len can't have a relationship with an extension of himself—yet he still has relationship needs—so he looks elsewhere. You see, symbiosis and relationship cannot coexist."

A lot of things thudded into place! I rushed home to dig out some notes I'd made from a John Sanford lecture years before. Sanford, both a clergyman and Jungian counselor, had shared insights that startled me with their clarity. Not wanting to lose them, I'd laboriously transcribed the whole recording of his talk. The audience that morning had been mostly women (though, ironically, Len had been with me and made the tape) and we'd hung on his words as though our very lives depended upon them.

> *Now about a man's psychology . . . he tends to see women as though they are all the same. While he remains at a very unconscious level—which is where most men are—he tends to see women either as mother, or, unconsciously, as an extension of himself. Or he sees her as filling his need for pleasurable gratification, which is another way of saying he sees her as mother. Now that's one of the things you're up against as women.*

He was speaking to us like a wise, caring older brother. I felt very sad as I recognized the truth of what he was confiding:

> *The expectations of the men in a woman's life tend to defeat her finding her own individual expression as a human being. If a woman starts to do this, it often brings her into conflict with the important men in her life and with that very culture which is dominated by masculine concepts and expectations. . . . It even brings her into conflict with her religion, for the feminine element is notably lacking in the Judaeo-Christian tradition.*[3]

He then described to us the rich, archetypal variations between women; indeed, we're not all the same![4] He urged us each to discover our own truth, to midwife that which was waiting to be born in us. Again, the message was "Grow or die."

I was learning much I needed to know as I gathered my strength. And I felt incredibly grateful for these few wise brothers who were champions of my developing personhood.

21

Breaking Through

Any breakthrough of new consciousness, though it may have been maturing for months or years out of sight, comes through a building up of tension which reaches a breaking point. If the man or woman stands firm with courage, the breakdown becomes a break-through into a surge of new life . . .[1]

Helen M. Luke

More days passed. I felt utterly torn apart, like I'd extricated one foot from the sticky symbiosis with Len but the other was still mired.

"I've got to finish getting free! I'm losing my hold on the most precious discovery of my life—myself!" I journaled.

One day I again sought peace for my troubled heart among the magnificent redwoods. But even there it eluded me, so I climbed the winding dirt road up through the forest to the top of the mountain where acres of terraced vineyards were wearing their new-spring green. I took off my clothes and lay naked under the sun's healing rays.

"God, what am I going to do?" I cried out. "Whatever am I going to do?"

After a while I descended the mountain still heavy and unresolved. I returned home to my familiar meditation chair near Christ's picture and desperately attempted to get quiet enough to hear the still, small voice within. Just as I'd about given up, I had my life's most dramatic experience of guidance. In words so authoritative I wondered if they were audible, I heard:

"Virginia, Len needs the security of his home. *You* are the one to move out." Before I could even gasp, "Where in the world shall I go?" the next direction was given. This time it came as a mental picture, an image of a widow I knew who lived about six blocks away. I'd not had contact with her since her husband's death two years before.

That was it! I knew that my anguished cry had been answered because all my turmoil lifted and a strange excitement took its place. Even before I was able to reach her by phone several hours later, I knew with absolute certainty that she'd have a place for me.

"Why yes," she said, very surprised at my request. "I moved out of my master bedroom for some long-term houseguests. They left last week, and everytime I thought about moving back in, something held me . . ." Oh, thank you, thank you, God.

That very evening I biked over to pay her a deposit on the room. My heart sang exultantly en route, "Joel Goldsmith, you were right! The Spirit does know our needs! The Spirit has gone before me and prepared the way."

And I'd been assured in that awesome, holy moment that not only were my needs known, but my beloved Len's as well. I was free, finally free, to leave in peace.

22

I Weep For My Child

People blossom in the surroundings of a woman who is in right relationship to herself, because then she is like the positive mother-goddess who makes corn grow. But if the relationship with her own inner self is wrong, she is more likely to emanate the effects of the death goddess Hecate, and put a blight of death over those around.[1]

Marie-Louise von Franz

One difficult task remained: telling Rolf that his mother was leaving home.

Our quiet, sensitive fourteen-year-old had been aware all winter that his family was in jeopardy. And that we were all too scared to talk much about it. He'd spent a lot of time behind the closed door of his room.

"There can't possibly be any nourishment in your home for that son of yours," Prescott had lamented one day. "You and Len are like frightened, clutching children, struggling emotionally to survive. I'm surprised you two chose to have children at all."

Through Prescott's eyes, I could see the emotional deprivation our kids had experienced. How incredibly sad I felt for all three, and especially, now, for Rolf. His brother and sister had escaped before the final, inevitable collapse. I wept for my remaining child.

Thank God for the few close sharing times I'd successfully initiated with Rolf that winter. He seemed so frustratingly hard to reach. And I was all strung out besides. But one day, about six weeks before I got my clear guidance to leave, I offered to give Rolf a nurturing, motherly massage on our new massage table. Instead of his usual "No thanks," he delighted me by accepting. Afterwards, feeling safe and loved, he was unusually self-disclosing.

"I'm so unhappy here, Mom. I've thought a lot about where I could go—maybe to live with Clark and his girlfriend, or hitchhike to the east coast to stay with Lynn and her friends. But I keep feeling like I'm supposed to be here for now."

"Then, if Dad and I separate, which one of us will you want to live with?" I asked as gently as possible.

"Please don't ask me to make that decision," he begged, swallowing hard. "If Dad moved out, you'd be crying all the time. And if you moved out, he'd sit around depressed, acting helpless and eating T.V. dinners." Either one was a horrendous prospect. Finally, sensing a decision might be necessary, he added, "I guess I'd stay with whomever kept this house. It's been my home all my life . . . Somehow I think I'd be able to protect myself from the bad vibes." How my heart went out to him.

As Rolf was growing up, we had come to respect his spiritual gifts and sensitivities. He often saw deeply, clearly into the heart of a matter. So I probed him at length as he made this prediction:

"Even if you and Dad separate, I know you'll get back together eventually."

"How can you sound so sure, Rolf?"

"I'm just positive. I don't know if it will take ten years or ten millenia. But you will. Because you and Dad are twin rays."

I pondered, "Is he picking up on that same 'union on inner planes' Michael said Len and I share, or does Rolf need this hope in order to survive his present pain?"

The day after my dramatic experience of guidance, I asked Rolf to have a cup of tea with me. "I just can't stay here any longer," I began tearfully. As I struggled to continue, he gently laid his hand over mine.

"Mom, I give you my blessing in whatever you have to do." I could scarcely believe the beauty of this young man. He'd reached down deep, through his own fear and grief, and found the grace to strengthen me.

Gratefully, I suggested we bike over to see my new home. "I want you to visit me here whenever you like. I'll continue taking my turns driving you to school, so I'll see you often." My attempt to encourage us both felt woefully feeble.

On the day of my move I consciously enlisted his help. I wanted so much for him to feel included in my new beginnings! But much later he told me,

"I remember nothing about that day; I guess I totally blocked it out. I recall that you and Dad were having problems—and then you were gone. I can't remember anything in between." Oh God, how I hurt to inflict pain that deep upon one I love.

I sought out Michael a couple months after my move and asked him his intuitions about Rolf. He replied thoughtfully to my sad queries.

"I see now why that child goes to his room and shuts the door. He has a hard time opening up to you people because he experiences the deception, the lie that you live. It grates in his guts. But since that's the consensual reality you and Len have created, Rolf has doubted himself. He has feared that there's something wrong with him." I felt stung and saddened. In those few words Michael had explained years of frustration in trying to be closer to this intelligent, sensitive boy.

Michael continued, "As you get more honest with yourself about your own feelings, more flowing, more in contact with yourself, you'll find a rich relationship developing with that son. But don't go looking for it; it'll come. He'll just respond to you when you're in that place. He can't help but open up to you."

I called Rolf the next day and invited him to take an evening walk with me. I gratefully told him, "There's nothing wrong with you, sweetie. You've been reacting to very real dishonesty and deception around you . . . and not understanding why you felt so awful. You're all right! You've been right on the whole time."

He was silently thoughtful as we walked. Then I felt something tight let go inside him. "You've brought me a lot of healing tonight," he said softly.

Belatedly, from my new space, I was starting to be an authentic friend to my lonely child.

23

"God, There's Just You And Me Now"

*A woman whose life seems destroyed by the end of
a marriage and whose basic sense of herself is rad-
ically shaken cannot pass simply into a new life and
a new identity . . . Unless a woman can begin to face
herself as an individual alone, not defined by having
someone to look after, she will be unable to utilize the
possibility offered by the crisis . . . to discover new
life.*[1]

Penelope Washbourn

The first lonely, scary night in my new room, I knelt down by
that strange bed and whispered, "God, there's just you and me
now."

I was one huge empty ache. That bed became my place of refuge
again and again. Whenever my fear paralyzed me, I turned the
electric blanket to high and curled up beneath it in the fetal
position, covering my head and all. When I could not cope, could
not even cry, could not pray, I mutely returned to that dark, warm
womb till I could function again.

Each time, however, a part of my consciousness seemed to stand
by as an observer, realizing, "Poor kid; that's the best she can do
today."

Spurred on by my loneliness, I found I was powerfully motivated
to grow beyond symbiotic needs—to prepare myself for the possibility of a real relationship with some fine man. How I yearned
to experience an emotionally satisfying love, one that sprang from
a sense of my own worth and potency. I knew I had a lot of
homework to do. And I knew I was absolutely committed to doing
it.

I must conquer my loneliness alone.
*I must be happy with myself or I have
    nothing to offer you.*

*Two halves have little choice but to join;
    and, yes, they do make a whole.
But two wholes, when they coincide . . .
That is beauty. That is love.*[2]

24

"Forgive Me, My Brothers"

*But if in your fear you would seek only love's peace
and love's pleasure,
Then it is better for you that you cover your
nakedness and pass out of love's threshing floor,
Into the seasonless world where you shall laugh,
but not all of your laughter, and weep, but not
all of your tears.*[1]

Kahlil Gibran

Die before death and resurrect now.

Sufi saying

"I need to keep learning a new way to relate to men," I realized. "A way that does not judge them nor attack their masculinity."

So often I'd seen men retreat as I aggressively challenged them on an intellectual level. I came on "macho" from my fear of having to deal with them as a woman.

Again I made this strong commitment to myself: "I want to be in touch with my femaleness even though it hurts. I *have* to live from the vulnerable beauty of my woman's soul, whatever the cost."

I quickly attracted opportunities to demonstrate my courageous resolve.

My first visit to Nan and Rob's ranch without Len was gut-wrenching. Through the years we had related to them primarily as a couple, treasuring their warm, wonderful friendship.

Nan and Rob live with their goats and chickens among the great oaks of the Sierra foothills. On the back of their property sits a small miner's cabin, a legacy from a previous owner. Nan made it lovely with colorful floor cushions and fragrant candles, and they named it "The Prayer Closet." It became a true center of light, a focal point for vital, flowing spiritual gatherings. Many lives have there been touched by transforming love. Len and I had led a retreat there not many months before.

But this morning I came to the Quiet Day gathering as a new widow. It was awkward for everyone who'd known me and Len as a spiritual leadership team. And no one could fail to see that behind my brave, tight smile I was feeling stripped and lost.

So we said little, but began to sing and worship, and the power of Love in that room gradually swelled to a mighty, healing crescendo. Broken open by its almost palpable presence, I silently agonized over my habitual, harsh judgment of men, and the pain I'd caused myself and others thereby. I desperately wanted to make confession to that dear group as a way of healing this pattern, of letting it go.

Mustering my courage, I crawled to the center, knelt there, and softly but firmly made this unusual request: "Will all the men come and pray for me?"

An electric charge swept the room; even the man dozing in the corner suddenly sat upright. It took only a moment for the several men present to recover from their surprise and begin to gather around me. They swept me into a comforting, collective bear hug and waited for me to speak. I was too humiliated to look into their eyes.

"Forgive me, my brothers," I began tearfully with my head bowed. "Forgive me for the way I judge men to try to avoid getting hurt, for the way I've included all of you in that judgment."

Their hearts remained open to me, and soon I felt immersed in a warm, healing pool of masculine love-power. My broken open heart soaked it up as a parched desert welcomes living water.

Rob spoke as he held me, "I also ask your forgiveness, my dear, for avoiding a closer friendship with you because I've been afraid of you." Obviously, in my softened, vulnerable state he feared me no longer.

Another spoke, "I ask your forgiveness for what we men have done to you." His words seemed to pour healing balm over wounds long suppurating within me.

The others spoke tenderly of their support; I could only respond, "Oh, my brothers," as I reached out gratefully to embrace each one.

The whole group fell silent for a long time after we returned to our places. Some of the women had joined me in quiet weeping. Then, one after another hesitantly acknowledged her own need for healing resolution with the masculine. This universal wound, individualized to some degree in each woman present, became, then, the focus of that blessed, prayer-filled day.

Nan's eyes shone that evening as she eagerly reported the image she'd seen while the men prayed for me. I had learned to respect her spontaneous spiritual sight.

"I saw a lifesized female mannequin. A sword appeared and easily sliced off its head, which rolled to the floor. Then the sword slit the mannequin open vertically, and, there, curled up inside was a *real woman* ready to be released!" Oh, thank you, God. Her vision more than confirmed the deep changes I felt occurring in me.

Rob beamed a benevolent, soul-brother smile upon me as I prepared to leave. "Now, my dear, you're ready for some positive male relationships."

"Yes!" I celebrated as I drove down the mountain. "My real woman is beginning to live!"

25

From Proud Lady To Real Woman

One is both grateful and resentful to the one who sets one on the path of evolution.[1]

Robert Johnson

As I drove home, I realized that the mannequin had received its decisive, shattering blow during those last humbling months with Len.

"If my husband had been undecided about whether he wanted to keep me or take another for his wife, I would have shattered, too," a wise friend said compassionately.

It was while my aggressive "Proud Lady" self was knocked to her knees in humiliation that the major breakthrough had occurred. Undoubtedly it took a blow that horrendous to shatter a defensive pattern so stubbornly entrenched. Thank God, I'd known to surrender to the refining fire. From deep within, my intuition told me, "Trust the wholeness process."

Only a total religious openness toward this spiritual principle that turns its creative aspect toward the feminine can enable the feminine to survive.[2]

Returning from one of those cold, lonely walks late at night, I had poured an original poem right out of my depths into my journal. It was the same night I'd discovered the beautiful manhood of Joseph in the Christmas crèche, and then stamped my foot at my negative animus, finally taking charge of my life. Now

I looked up that remarkable poem, and again I felt the power of metamorphosis explode in my body.

A Proud, Proud Lady In Crisis And Transformation

I am a proud, proud lady.
Offend me not!
Or you shall feel the bite of many clever strategies
　designed to make you squirm, you worm!
I am a proud, proud lady
Learned in the fine art of manipulation and control,
With intuition and other clever ones, my teachers,
And many lifetimes, my bitter schoolroom.
My words convey, "How dare you!"
However they're expressed;
And when I'm toppled from my throne
　(and that's happened many times)
I bring down as many with me as I can.
And my wrath against those who've cleverly betrayed me,
And beaten me at my own game, is terrible.

Now I am in crisis, hurting,
Sickened in alarm,
As I confront my haughty visage in the mirror of
　circumstances.
"What have I accomplished?" now I ask.
The ones I loved and needed have slipped through my net.
The ones I manipulated and controlled have cried, "No
　more!"
And found a way to extricate themselves, in part,
Yet still bearing scars inflicted by my overbearing self.
Oh God Within, I come to thee, shattered, bleeding and
　repentant,
With prayer arising from my deepest soul.
Bowed and humbled, I cry out: "Break me totally! Free me
　now from this self-defeating pattern.
Let my willful strength now be transformed
Into the strength of loving and serving Thee.

(My Journal)

I had paid the price to live.

26

"You'll Meet Someone Upon The Path"

Psychology . . . cannot rescue us without the help of religion . . . Only a genuinely religious psychology is adequate.[1]

Fritz Kunkel

At the time I separated from Len I was in the home stretch on my master's degree in counseling psychology. Pointing toward this immediate goal eased the trauma of losing my family. I threw myself into my studies and discovered that my newly-liberated real woman brought fresh energy to everything I did.

One evening in "Psychosynthesis"[2] class we chose partners to learn a guided imagery technique. I lay on the hard floor of the darkened classroom with my eyes closed, little knowing a profound experience awaited me.

My partner instructed, ". . . Now leave the sunny meadow for the deep forest. You'll meet someone or something along the path."

To my surprise, a handsome, bronzed American Indian stepped from behind a tree wearing only a loincloth and a headband with two feathers. My initial fear dissolved as I felt something familiar about him. Where had I known him? Soon we were embracing as openly as children.

"I am so happy to find you!" I told him, my heart strangely warm with joy.

My partner asked, "What does he want from you?"

"Oh! To show me the things of nature which he knows so well. Right now he takes me to the trout pool . . . He wants me to come here to be with him often."

"Now become the Indian. What quality does he represent?"

"Ah! An incredible balance of earthiness and reverence for the Great Spirit." He dug his bare toes into the forest mulch with such delight. "Why, he's an earthy, grounded mystic!" There by the stream we again embraced devotedly, passionately.

"Ask him if he'd like to climb the nearby mountain with you."

"Yes, he wants to . . . We pause now and then along the climb for him to show me the wild flowers."

"When you reach the top, look up and see the face of the Wise One in the sun," my partner continued.

"Oh yes! We both see it. And my Indian has raised his arms in reverence to the Great Spirit . . . Now we stand with our arms around each other, gazing upward. We love each other so!" Standing there upon that sunlit height, I passionately desire sexual union with this beloved. Easily, we join our bodies there in total, upright embrace.

"Ask the Wise One in the sun to come down on the mountaintop to be with you. . . . What happens?"

"He beams a radiant smile upon us. He tells us, 'I am so glad you have found each other. It is good that you are together.' "

When it is time to come back down the mountain, I do not feel my Indian and me part. My heart stays warm with a healing glow for hours afterwards, attesting to our inner oneness.

"Tonight," I wrote gratefully in my journal, "I met a beloved part of myself. He put me in touch with my natural earth energy and joined it sweetly to my spirit.[3] I feel so much more whole. Thank God, I am beginning to experience the mystical inner marriage."

27

"Mother, I've Come"

In innumerable counselling situations the tragic alienation of women from their femininity becomes clear. . . . Before a woman can safely pursue her goals with the true masculine discrimination that will bring her to maturity, she must first learn to recognize and to value the nature of the principle which is dominant in her by the fact of her sex. I am not denying the obvious truth that there is a great difference in the balance of the male and female elements in each person, but, whether the difference is great or small, nature tips the scales at our conception one way or the other, and no growth or transformation is ever possible until we have accepted the facts.[1]

Helen M. Luke

My newly-released real woman was ready to taste the nourishing nectar of life. She was very, very hungry.

During that last six months with Len, Michael had referred me to "a therapist who's got it together as a woman." I discovered that I was afraid of her! I could not weep in her presence, and since I was full of pain from the then recent death of my mother coupled with the crumbling state of my marriage, I desperately needed to feel safe enough to cry.

"You still need to get your mothering from a man," she said kindly at our third session. "You see, your father was the more feeling parent, so you looked to him for mothering even though, being a man, he wasn't equipped to give it. I want you to work with my colleague, Prescott, for awhile." So that was how his healing presence had entered my life.

I admitted to myself, "No wonder I'm so devastated at the prospect of losing Len. I've tried to get from him both fathering and mothering."

I trusted Prescott immediately. I explained to him that first session: "My Mother always said with a frown, 'Don't cry! It hurts my ears.'"

"Hell!" he exploded indignantly. "Bring me some pictures of this woman."

As we looked at them together, he pointed out what I'd chosen to forget. While I was growing up, Mom was an unhappy person. (Did she regret the decision to give up her teaching career to belatedly have children?) Her face was stern, her eyes dull, her body stiff and matronly. "She certainly lacked earth-mother energy," he accurately observed. "She looks like she could have taken on a whole gang of gorillas and kept everyone of them in line."

I didn't know whether to laugh or cry. But he continued soberly, "I'd have either shrunk up or become violent with a mother like that."

"Mother had a lot of integrity," I objected. "And she became warmer, even jolly, in her later years. Her grandchildren adored her."

"That did you no good," he retorted.

I pondered that disturbing exchange for a long time. For I could see both qualities he'd mentioned within myself. I had indeed contracted, afraid of full, spontaneous participation in life. And my barely suppressed violence often surfaced in nightmares and in tearing up my own chronically itchy skin. I seemed to have turned a lot of my violence in upon myself, though others close to me had also suffered at my hands.

"Why did I choose for my mother a frustrated woman who couldn't model a conscious, feminine way of engaging the world?" I anguished. "And a father whose manhood could not support her in finding that?" Then I recalled Michael's revelations of the past-life affect patterns I'd brought in with me. I simply could not plead "innocent victim."

One day Prescott surprised me with these words: "I want you to have a massage from my friend, Norinda. She has the earth-mother energy your mother lacked, and I want you to feel what it's like."

A blessed synchronicity prepared me for that experience. The day before the scheduled massage I had another healing encounter in Psychosynthesis class at the university. The "Wise Teacher" I was instructed to find in the guided imagery turned out to be a beatific gray-haired woman! In Eastern religious teachings I had read of the Divine Mother, and in ancient European cultures, of the goddess. From Jungian writings I'd learned that a woman's Self is symbolized in feminine form. But it mattered little who she was; I was so profoundly comforted by her presence.

"I will be with you through all these changes," her compassionate eyes assured me.

Lovely Norinda laid her earth-mother hands upon me the next day. I was amazed to experience what Prescott had extolled. As she stroked my back firmly, yet gently, her warm, nourishing energy flowed into me and seemed to fill me. I felt like the prodigal returning home—not to the Father but to the Mother.

Her loving countenance of the day before filled my inner vision again. "Mother, I've come," I breathed. "I've been away too long. Here I am, here I am!" My heart sang it over and over in grateful refrain.

Norinda gazed at me in utter delight as she finished. "You look younger!" I have no doubt that my face was shining. For my aching, hungry inner child was filled to overflowing. I felt reconnected and reborn.

28

From "Virginia" To "Helene"

To him that overcometh will I give to eat of the hidden
manna . . . and a new name . . .

Revelations 11:17

I received another joyous indication of the long distance already
traveled. It had happened during the last month with Len.

I awoke one morning from an astonishing dream. In it, a woman
I greatly respect in real life (a minister's wife) had counseled me
thus:

"Do you know you were a proud lady in the Elizabethan era?"
she asked. No, I did not, but "proud lady" had an all-too-familiar
ring even in the dream. She then sketched out my present lifetime
with Len, scolding me gently for many mistakes. But she ended
emphatically, "The name Virginia is too harsh for you now. Your
new name is Helene." And I awoke in wonderment!

I phoned her that day to ask, "Do you know you gave me a new
name in a dream last night?" She did not seem surprised. "You
must have represented my higher Self," I told her. "Helene is not
a name I would consciously have chosen; the only Helene I've
known was the kid next door as I grew up and she was a real
brat!"

I continued, "I've looked up the name's derivation. Helene is
a form of Helen, which comes from the Greek word for light:
Helios. My dictionary goes on: 'Helen (of Troy) was reputed to be
the most beautiful woman in the world.' I believe I have just been
named 'Beautiful Woman of Light!'"

"Yes!" she agreed. "As you meditate, I suggest you claim that
name. Let it be a symbol of your new beingness: not your parents'
daughter, not your husband's wife, not your children's mother.
But a brand new child of God!" Her words touched me; she and
her husband had been a faithful prayer support during my dark
night of the soul. How appropriate that she be the bearer of good
tidings in this, my unforgettable dream!

I told Len about it also. He pleased me by addressing me once
as "Helene." His smile was bemused but not mocking. It is important to me to remember that he acknowledged my new name.

I took this symbol of transformation quietly inside and held it
there in the fertile darkness of my psyche. It grew within for over

a year. Then, in the fullness of time I brought it forth and stepped into its greater, yet softer, light.

29

"Blessed Are We Among Women"

There has to be earth as well as seed before new life is created. The masculinity of the spirit is meaning-less unless it enters a feminine container. . . . If we can rediscover in ourselves the hidden beauty of this receptive devotion . . . then we shall be women again out of whose earth the light may shine.[1]

Helen M. Luke

I continued to find models for my heroic journey in all kinds of unexpected places. For one, in the little Catholic church nearby.

I'm convinced that spiritual reality is the native turf of every woman. Some say that a woman lives close to the Holy Grail castle and enters it almost at will. But, oh my, it's not that simple! For I had tragically lost touch with the nourishing soul-depths of "home," my life becoming a weary desert indeed. Now I was learning that the journey back requires a special, vulnerable kind of heroism.

One lonely afternoon I got on my bike to again seek the solace of a neighborhood church open for prayer. I gratefully entered its worshipful silence and, in my brokenness, found myself taking another significant leap in reconnecting with my feminine Self. I share this profound experience with you, recorded in my journal just as it happened:

I surprise myself a bit, choosing this small Catholic church in my hours of need. For I have valued my Protestant roots in spite of their serious lack of a feminine spiritual model. I smile to remember that I might have been born in a Methodist pew had not Mother's sudden labor prompted her speedy exit from choir practice to the hospital!

Here I sit in the pew of a different faith; now the creative pangs of new birth, new beginnings, are my own. And I acknowledge that it's the Mary-energy I feel in this quiet place which draws me back again and again. Her life-sized statue has been skillfully sculpted with a caring, compassionate face. I first discovered this one sad day when I drew close to her outstretched arms and knelt before her. Her face became, in that moment, the living symbol of the Divine Mother, the tender, comforting, unconditional love I was needing. The burden I had brought was released along with my tears as I gazed up at her, childlike, and let my spontaneous prayer pour forth.

Today I come to her as woman to woman, younger sister to older. A prayer I once read and memorized serves me well: "Hail Mary, full of grace, the Lord is with thee, and with me in my way; so, blessed are we among women. Pray for me now, for I am beginning to know what you know. Help me to know it fully, to bring it to birth."[2]

How my heart is nourished by communion with the image of God in the feminine! As the church gradually darkens with fading sunset, my eyes are held by the flickering prayer candles at her feet.

"What is it you know that I am only beginning to know?"

And answering thoughts arise, "Most of all, the power of receptive devotion. The power of a yearning, yielded heart, open to the highest one can conceive. It's the soft strength of yin, the creative feminine spiritual principle, and it complements and completes yang, the creative masculine principle."

I ponder Mary's long-ago encounter with Gabriel. "You were woman, too. When Gabriel came to tell you that you were chosen to receive the seed of God and bear the incarnate Christ, you expressed fear and unbelief, perhaps even dismay. Was not your God compromising you in the eyes of your betrothed and your community? I don't know how long you struggled with these very human, very woman considerations. But you broke through!

"Behold the handmaid of the Lord; let it be to me according to your word." And this was no begrudging assent to your destiny! "My soul magnifies the Lord and my spirit rejoices in God my Savior."[3]

Now grateful tears arise as my whole body quickens. I have struck gold in my yearning search for inner wholeness. And it does not matter to me whether the Bible record is historically accurate or not. For my spirit bears witness to the truth of Mary's response. I am feeling a Mary-part in me, hungering for, and yes, capable of the courageous devotion with which a woman can embrace her unique destiny.

I choose so to do!

30

"Let The City Burn And Don't Look Back"

Divorce is a process, not an event.

Unknown

At the time I moved out I agreed to evaluate my relationship with Len at the end of the summer, six months hence. He and I even discussed attending a conference together in Colorado, the place where we'd met and married.

But I soon discovered that my relief in being out of the home far outweighed my loneliness. When I dropped by to carpool Rolf or get my mail, I felt heavily oppressed by that house and everything in it. I reluctantly acknowledged in my journal, "I see that I can never live there again. . . . I cannot slow my growth to wait for him; I *must* move on. Dear God, help me do so with kindness toward Len every step of the way."

Len's eyes filled with tears each time he saw me. He was feeling a great sense of loss, and I was touched—in spite of my anger—by his belated grieving. "He is finally getting the message that I'm leaving him for good," I wrote with my own sad, frightened tears streaming.

I had not consulted with Michael for over a year. Three times during those darkest months of my life I had compulsively dialed him to schedule an appointment, primarily for reassurance. But each time my spiritual intuition seemed to override, suggesting, "Don't abort this refining fire process. Take one day at a time drawing from the Source of strength within you." So I had cancelled those appointments. But two months after I separated from Len, I got a clear inner nudge to see Michael. I was ripe for another big change and needed him to help catalyze it.

He could see how scared and shaky I was in spite of my pluck. "That was a healthy move you made," he commented on my change of residence. "But I'm sensing that Len doesn't want to let you go. You're a secure place, and in many ways you two did a lot of positive growing together and a lot of serving the light. You each got to the place where you needed to split; but *he's not letting you go!* He has a lot of psychic tentacles coming into your lower centers, tying you up. You need to mobilize your rage and literally shake him loose. Especially if you're wanting relationships with other men."

Then Michael fell silent and closed his eyes. When we resumed talking, my head felt remarkably clearer.

"What happened?" I asked.

"You're starting to hear me now. Len was so permeating your energy that I had to go in and clear a space just to talk to you. I literally had to push him out mentally. And I felt like he was coming at me with an axe, tantrum-like, because I'm wanting to tell you things you need to hear to be your own person again."

"Wow! Getting free is vastly more complicated than just moving out," I realized.

Michael went on, "He's a powerful mentalist. And he doesn't always use it with the right intentions."

"Yes, I know. Sometimes I go around thinking Len's thoughts. One day at the university I realized I'd heard a whole lecture through his ears. I was disgusted as I confronted myself afterwards, 'Hey, I'm a forty-four-year-old woman. What did *I* think of that lecture. And how come I give so much of my power away to my man?' "

Michael continued, "Now you're breaking away from him emotionally, but he still contains your energy on mental and psychic levels. You need to find out that you have your own mind apart from him . . . He doesn't want you to get free because that throws him back on having to deal with himself, with his own feminine side. He's done an incredible job of avoiding that for a long time."

Then Michael put me on the spot. "I see that you've got a lot of letting go still to do, too. You're still hoping that you and this man will get together again somewhere out there. Listen, you've got to go live your life *totally for you* without any hope or intention of that. When you can do that—and he can do that—then you're free to meet again *if* you so choose. But as long as you're doing your growing toward that end, you've not really let go." I felt very sad. Yes, I was hoping. Though still smarting over Len's betrayal, I loved him.

He continued gently, "It will take some time. Don't deny your desire for that, but when that hope wants to let itself go, and you want to go and live your own life, do it! Let your bridges burn behind you! Let him, that house, everything, burn behind you! Even your children, because the greatest gift you can give them is your own liberation. Like Lot, let the whole city burn and just follow the Lord. Follow the light that's been drawing you on. And DON'T LOOK BACK!"

31

"It Is Finished"

Aye, you shall be together even in the silent memory of God.[1]

Kahlil Gibran

The next morning I awoke with a clear mind. I knew what I wanted and needed to do.

I called Len and asked him to come over. There in my new room, I shared with him much of what Michael had told me. He listened intently, for he had great respect for Michael's gifts. Finally, I summed up:

"Len, I'm asking you to let me go. I want your tentacles out of me. And I want us to proceed with a divorce."

I saw beads of perspiration gather on his upper lip. He sat stunned for awhile. Then his face registered a deep sadness. But that finally gave way to resignation, even the beginning of relief. For had we not both known all along that we had to set each other free?

Within the week we agreed upon a property settlement and began the divorce. I was frequently weepy after each step we took toward the dissolution of our long marriage. We had loved each other; we had hated each other. For a quarter-century we had been best friends and worst enemies. This was the man who had deflowered me, who had impregnated me and stood beside me through three laborings of childbirth. We had shared pride in our beautiful children. We had done a lot of growing together, some happy, much of it in pain. This man, this marriage, had indelibly imprinted my life.

It would take me years to process the marriage, to distill its essence, to emotionally let it go. It would be like peeling an onion, layer after tearful layer. Even as I write, this is being completed.

We did not know when we filed for divorce that it would become final on our twenty-fifth wedding anniversary! This synchronicity underscored what I sensed life was telling us:

"It is finished."

32

Too Easily Replaced

There's no way you can deny that he's still on the planet. You're not out of relationship to him; it's just been transformed into something else. You're both expressions of the one Life, and one part of the God-force cannot refuse to relate to another part of itself.

Michael

Len succeeded in letting me go, it seemed to me, by quickly plugging into someone else. I want to tell you about it.

Within a few days of my request for a divorce, he called Saralynn to reactivate their long-distance romance. She agreed to a secret rendezvous which must have been a success, for soon he went back to the midwest to help her separate from her husband and bring her three young children to California to live. She got a job and an apartment nearby and Len entered immediately into an exclusive relationship with her. Soon he'd taught her the rudiments of assisting as co-leader in his groups.

"He has already replaced me in both the bedroom and the business," I complained to Prescott. "I'm amazed and confused by how easy that was for him."

"I can see how you'd feel too easily replaced."

It was Saralynn whom Len took to Colorado for the conference. I was surprised to learn he'd taken her to the campus and the nearby church where he and I had married. He got a tension headache there; she was understanding.

Before Saralynn gave up her job and moved in with Len, he took a pottery course and discovered that he had natural talent as a potter. I was happy for him that he made that excursion into his earth, his feminine side.

One day when I phoned Rolf I heard Saralynn's children playing noisily in the background. The sound of children's voices echoing in that familiar house sent me searching into my memories. "My God," it suddenly hit me, "Len's trying to turn the clock back ten years!"

I remembered him telling me once, "I was so cut off from my feelings when our children were growing up. I feel sad that I missed so much." Was he trying to make up for that loss? But Saralynn's children had a lot of ambivalence about their "new

73

Daddy" and this grieved Len, of course.

Len and Saralynn married. I was relieved when he returned to his original engineering profession in order to support his large, new family. After a year his firm moved him to southern California, and he and Saralynn made a fresh start in a home that did not contain the energy of our marriage. They bought a spacious home complete with backyard pool. Len wrote to former clients, "I'm amazed to discover that I have everything I've always wanted." Eventually Len and Saralynn had their own little son, the apple of their eye.

Our grown children enjoy visiting their Dad and his second family. They value Len as a loving father and friend. Through their eyes, I sense that he is weathering the continual challenges of step-fatherhood and a new baby at fifty-one. Len seems to feel safely supported by Saralynn's love. She is a kind, intelligent woman who finds her natural foci in her family and her church.

I am humbled to realize that she can do for him what I could not. Yet I have not resented her. But only gradually have I found the grace to celebrate the fact that Len is blossoming in his second marriage in ways he could not in ours.

No wonder Len and I were destroying each other! Our needs had become drastically different. It is obvious why the Spirit of more abundant life drew Its sword inexorably between us, setting us both free.

Divorce does not always mean that a marriage has been a failure. There are some marriages in which, though both partners have been true to their vows, and have grown through the years into a more adult love, a time may yet come when unlived parts of their personalitites are striving to become conscious. A situation may then arise in which it becomes obvious that if they remain together, these two, who basically love and will always love each other, will regress into sterility and bitterness if they do not have the courage to accept the suffering of parting. Their quest for wholeness may then demand *that they ignore the outer laws of church and society in order to be true to the absolutely binding inner vow "to love and to cherish from this time forward." One does not have to be living with a person—or even to see him ever again—in order to love and cherish through everything. A conscious acknowledgement of failures, an*

74

unshaken devotion to the love which sets free, can turn a divorce into a thing of positive beauty, an experience through which a person may bring out of the suffering a purer love to all future meetings. The divorce is then a sacrificial not a destructive act and the original marriage may remain in the deepest sense, procreative to the end of life.[1]

33

Goody-Goody Girl Vs. Spiritual Woman

. . . for a woman who tries to play the role of the good wife, the call of her own development may come in the form of breaking the marriage vows . . . A woman . . . realizes that for her, love and spirit are mixed together. . . . To follow love may mean, then, to follow what is disturbing and anxious, to go the downward road into the undifferentiated layers of being, not allowing her so-called virtue to separate her from others or inwardly to estrange her from herself.[1]

Ann Belford Ulanov

It was my season for being stripped—stripped of ego defenses, of family support systems, of extraneous material possessions. I found myself dropping ballast in order to travel light on the next stage of my journey. With shaky steps, I ventured into the discovery of who and what I was apart from all these. What an exhilarating process—finding myself! I was reminded of Jesus' parable of the treasure hidden in the field which the person sold everything to obtain.

Even with my increasing self-knowledge, I was still distrustful of my own deep impulses where they conflicted with my previous, rigid value system. So, burdened by confusion and aching needs, I again sought out Michael for his transformative wisdom.

"What's wrong?" I sighed.

He minced no words. "You've got a lot of needs as a woman that aren't being met. But you're not wanting to partake of what's available to you. You are holding out for the 'big whammy,' thinking that now that you're free the cosmic man is going to come into your life and you'll feel like the cosmic woman. But you're not there yet! If a man came along who was totally present and he wanted to connect with you, you wouldn't recognize him. You're still fragmented and confused, and any relationship you have with a man is going to reflect that. He'll be no more present than you are."

"I sure feel hungry for *some* masculine energy in my life," I acknowledged.

"Well, allow yourself to have what's available to you now. You've been waiting for the whole dinner when all you're ready for is a good lunch!"

He went on, "You're avoiding relationships with men by pushing them away because they don't measure up to what you think you should have. Men are going to start coming into your life soon, and until you let yourself interact with those who are being drawn to you, and work with that energy so it can be transformed, you're not going to go beyond that point in your growth. Is that clear?" I nodded weakly. "Well, allow yourself just to feel the energy between you and a man, your feelings, your heart's innocence, and flow with that without making judgments about where it will go or how that man compares to Len or your ideal. Even if it's just a one night affair, you've asked for it on some level. So stop denying yourself the things you need to grow as a woman."

"But Michael!" I now vehemently objected. "How could I possibly reconcile that with my spiritual path? I've been through hell these past several years, and it was only by surrendering to the God-Source of strength within me that I've survived. You know that!"

Sensing my honest confusion, he spoke patiently as he shared a profound teaching that I've returned to many times.

"O.K. Let me give you a model: Creation has two movements, like breathing. One is the downward spiral, the descent of spirit into matter; the other, the rise of matter back to spirit." He quickly sketched the arrows on a paper napkin.

"You're still experiencing the lessons of the earth. Each lesson you surrender to liberates that much more of you to go back up again. I respect your longing to go up. But there are still parts of you needing to come down first. Because the only way to ascend unto God is to descend into yourself. Remember that the great mystics in their yearning for God recognize how much they're 'sinners' because their growth process takes them right into their darkness? Purgation of the darkness can only come from experiencing it."

"Yes, I can see that."

"Well, now realize that the Universe is really a giant behavior modification system, helping us discover what works and what hurts. Surrender, then, to who and what you are—even surrender your concept of how you're supposed to evolve—and just keep looking toward the light while accepting whatever you're doing. You're needing self-acceptance instead of self-denial."

His words, though strange, rang true. I found I was eager to hear on.

"Accepting yourself as a being of light is accepting your humanity," he told me. "You are moving both up *and* down right now, and there's still a lot of you that needs to live on the earth. *All* actions are in the light, a part of God's Plan inevitably taking you back to wholeness."

Now he sensed my readiness for some harsh, yet healing words.

"Listen, lady, what you've seen yourself to be as a spiritual being is based on the goody-goody girl game you've played since childhood. It's a huge mind-fuck which you use to deny yourself in a very toxic way. It would probably make Christ weep! *The last thing He wants you to do is deny your own fulfillment as a woman, because it's through your womanhood that you'll realize your spiritual nature.*" Pointing to my body, he reminded me, *"This* is the temple."

Finally I was beginning to understand the mystery of incarnation. I flashed back to the time Michael had spoken to Len of such things. "Beware of the spiritual trip," he'd told him. "Cutting off from your lower centers is *not* mastery. Let yourself be a man living on the earth in a physical body, and the spiritual nature will rise out of that base. Manhood *cannot* be bypassed in favor of Christhood."

Now I was starting to appreciate the challenges and opportunities of our souls' "laboratory of earth experience." Here we are to wed earth and heaven, flesh and spirit. Both must be honored and joined in wholeness. We are to be "spiritually active within the world and worldly active within the Spirit."[2]

That day with Michael was another turning point on my way. My spirit bore witness to the appropriateness of his counsel for that season in my growth.

Only by going down, *not by striving upwards, would she find herself. She must plunge into the river of life* unconditionally, *risking mistakes or failure . . . Only by trusting herself to the unknown, both in her outer life and in her own hidden depths, would she find her unique way.*[3]

I winced as I realized that acting upon Michael's counsel would surely cause bewilderment, even condemnation from my conservative religious friends. (Yes, and it stung.) But I was amazed to feel the strength of my commitment to my woman's journey in spite of its surprising twists and turns. Love, which I desired above everything, required my willingness to risk all. And by now there was simply no turning back.

34

"My God Has Been Too Small"

The ancients were not cursed with the puritanical split between earth and the holy.[1]

Helen M. Luke

At my next therapy session with Prescott, he added some psychological insights to Michael's mystical ones.

"Adolescence is a time of experimentation—a time for avoiding a too-early committed relationship. You're needing to explore the world and yourself in it," Prescott advised.

Adolescence! I knew I had fearfully squelched my awakening adolescent energies in my youth. I had married at twenty, proud that I was still "untarnished"—but a dependent child, emotionally.

I was now convinced from my own studies in psychology that each developmental stage has to be experienced. When a stage is denied and repressed, it doesn't go away; instead, its life-force builds up a charge in the unconscious while awaiting its opportunity to be lived. My rigid value system, borrowed from my puritanical parents (and indeed, my generation), had prevented me from experimenting with life at a more appropriate age. How humbling to now consciously enter adolescence at mid-life after twenty-five years of marriage! Appropriate or not, I was in it.

"I've been having very sexual dreams," I told Prescott one day. "Generally, with older men. Guess I still have a big need for fathering."

"No," he objected. "You're opening up sexually. Your growth has been true during these months of therapy. Your body has told you something in these dreams, and you've interpreted them—as you often do—in a squelching way. I don't like the way you lay numbers on yourself."

He explained further, "With Len you never really had the experience of a lover because your healthy woman's passion was so messed up with all that symbiotic schmuck. Why, you may need fifteen lovers in order to experience the whole gamut of clutching, not clutching, letting go." Good grief! Apparently the shock I felt showed on my face, for he added, "Yes, it may take that many before you finally get free to express the beauty of love and sexuality as a woman."

> *The phenomenon of the divorced man or woman unconsciously marrying a carbon copy (either physically or emotionally) of his former mate is well known. . . . The period of experimentation following a divorce is tailor-made for discovering—and breaking—patterns from the past.*[2]

That night I got quiet as I watched the stars twinkle through my bedroom window. Before I slept, I wrote:

"I'm almost envious tonight of my fundamentalist Christian friends. For them, right and wrong, black and white, are so sharply defined. It's not to be that simple for me. My God has been too small. . . . My Lord, is it You guiding my unfolding sexuality?"

35

Finding My Wood Nymph

> *For most women very considerable life experience is needed to grasp the truth for which they had been completely unprepared: that for the whole woman there is no possible cleavage between spirit and body, for it is in her body that her spirit dwells . . . Once understood, her inhibiting fear that man only wants her body vanishes into thin air. She can abandon herself as never before in the physical encounter, for she knows that if he can meet her in the body he cannot fail also to find her spirit.*[1]
>
> Irene Claremont de Castillejo

"How I ache for someone to hold me close and penetrate my flesh deeply this night," I acknowledged in my journal. As that aching need to love and be loved grew more intense, I knew I'd have to act upon it. I was grateful to Michael and Prescott for giving me a context in which to do so with self respect. Still, I feel quite vulnerable as I open my life in these pages.

I was simply not ready for any relationship that smacked of commitment. So I began having fantasies of F.P., the man I'd had the intense affair with six years earlier. "Would he still find me attractive?" I worried in front of my mirror.

I decided to risk it, and sent him the general announcement of my divorce. I requested of friends and clients in that letter, "I ask for your love and prayers as I find my way as a productive single woman."

F. P. called the day he got it! I was thrilled. "When?" he asked enthusiastically. "When can we get together?"

I began to feel alive as I anticipated our rendezvous and searched for a seductive, black nightie.

The day finally arrived. F. P. brought me the welcome gift of his passion and his tenderness. How I needed both! And he did still find me beautiful! But in spite of my torrid fantasies, my love-making responses were slow and disappointing that day. As I wept in his arms I felt the full weight of my shattered, needy woman. I'd limped out of my marriage feeling uncherished, even unrecognized by my husband as a person apart from his needs. F.P.'s passion and respectful, tender concern brought the beginning of healing to this wounded woman. Then his work took him abroad for several months.

The next romance took me by surprise. Through my love of music I reconnected with a talented musician I'd known professionally for several years. Now I was struck with his earthy, wholesomely sexual male energy; I'd never felt so much of that in a man before! I found myself powerfully pulled toward him; and his twinkling, flirtatious eyes revealed that he was also aware of the strong chemistry between us. I knew he was married and had children, but obviously affairs were part of his lifestyle. I found myself most willing!

But I wasn't sure how to let him know. It was, after all, a professional relationship. "I hope he'll call me," I fretted to Prescott.

"Well, how come you're giving the man all the power to decide whether there's to be a relationship? Why don't you call him?"

My hand trembled and my heart pounded as I dialed him at

work. "Nick, I'm not going to be coy with you," I said trying to sound composed. "I'd like to see you."

"Beautiful!" he exulted. "When can I come over?"

Through Nick I discovered delightful new joys of man-woman sharing. "He's the living embodiment of my earthy Indian in the forest imagery," I realized. "The inner lover has now manifested in the outer! He's earthy, playful, sweet," I journaled happily. "He unpretentiously celebrates his maleness! He delights in my femaleness! He evokes in me a natural, passionate abandonment. I've discovered my wood nymph self! Oh, I like her!"

"That man has his feet on the ground," Prescott said approvingly as he witnessed my rapid flowering.

In a few weeks, however, Nick told me he didn't want to be tied down by our affair. I was obviously more invested in it than he, for I'd given him my eager heart as well as my body. I was crushed as he became more casual, dropping in when his work brought him to my area. We began to miss connections. I nastily complained to him about taking me for granted, and secretly decided that I didn't like the powerlessness of being a mistress, of being second instead of first.

Finally I admitted to myself in my journal, "I'm doing my grief-work for this sweet season of being Nick's lover. My drippy nose, my wheezy chest—and my horribly empty gut—remind me of the death of my marrriage. But I see it's a mini-death compared to before."

Now I flashed on Prescott's prophecy with greater comprehension: "You may need fifteen lovers to run the whole gamut of clutching, not clutching, letting go, to finally get free . . . " Nick had been my teacher as well as my lover.

After some summer travel, including a restful month in Hawaii as guest of my sister, I found my spirit renewed. As fall began I was emotionally ready to risk a love affair with an eligible, fiftyish bachelor I was introduced to at church. This quickly became a powerful relationship.

"I've never met a woman I'd consider spending the rest of my life with until I found you," William told me as his honest, adoring blue eyes held mine. As I quickly became the major focus of his life, I felt marvelously, incredibly special. His warm, attentive energy brought deep healing to my woundedness.

Bouquets of red roses now continually perfumed my room, and candlelit cuisine was my frequent fare. It was all heady wine for a woman who'd been at rock bottom only one year before.

36

Guided One Step At A Time

*. . . waiting [is] an essential positive quality of the
feminine. . . . No woman as woman can plan her future. She can plan a career, but as woman she can
only wait for the future to unfold itself.*[1]

Irene Claremont de Castillejo

*For a journey in consciousness, the map you seek
exists within you and unfolds as you travel.*[2]

Henry Reed

Empowered by William's loving devotion, I moved step by step
into my true work.

But I'd already scored some huge victories over fear before I
met him. I told Michael the dream I had in my lonely room a few
days after separating from Len:

"I'm at a train station; I've bought my ticket for the trip. A man
sneaks up behind me and grabs my purse. Gone is my ticket, gone
is my money, gone is my identification (my identity). I feel utterly
wiped out." My fears couldn't have been portrayed more suc-
cinctly. "I'm scared," I told Michael.

"But there's a flow of energy waiting to work with you! There
are some women in your pattern who will be more than happy
to help you start anew because of their respect for you. You'll find
a lot of women drawn to you as you take the lead, and you'll be
able to share with deep empathy for what a woman is going
through because you know the struggle yourself. You'll be only
one to four steps ahead of them, no more. After each step you'll
turn around and say, 'Follow; this is what I've learned.' And you've
got to keep moving."

*. . . the journey was always toward "home" . . . toward
the place where, through her relation to the Earth
Mother and to the Wise Woman, she was initiated
into womanhood, which is the home of the feminine
principle, a home that not every woman finds.*[3]

Soon the pieces started falling into place just as Michael predicted. One morning I awoke with the inspiration to ask my lan-

dlady if I could rent her unoccupied third bedroom for a counseling room. She grinned at me delightedly. "I awoke this very morning knowing you'd ask me that. Yes, of course." She was employed downtown, so the house was virtually mine all day. I furnished that cheerful yellow room with colorful cushions and green growing plants. It felt like me! A few former clients began coming, plus an occasional new one.

By fall, when I was ready to offer my first women's weekend workshop, another widow-friend gave me the use of her beach house overlooking beautiful Monterey bay.

I looked up an old acquaintance who now directed a neighborhood branch of the YWCA. She let me teach a class for her women there; I called it, "Exploring a Woman's Inner World." These were small but solid beginnings.

I was not earning enough to support myself and that worried me a lot. For months, every time I sat down to balance my checkbook I burst into tears. But I pushed through my fears of using some of the modest cash settlement from my divorce, realizing in calmer moments that life had provided it for exactly that purpose.

With my M. A. diploma finally in my hand, I pondered my next career steps. Should I invest additional years in a Marriage and Family counseling specialty? That path felt dead, without heart. Should I go for a Ph.D.? No; I yearned to put my talents to work, not for more academic study.

One quiet, prayerful night I got a strong inner sense, "Just be about the Father-Mother's business. You will be guided one step at a time."

Little did I dream of the adventures that lay ahead on that unfolding Path.

"I'm Afraid I'll Marry Him And Afraid I Won't"

The image of a man and a woman who love each other is one of our most beautiful ongoing ways to learn about the inward love relationships of the human soul.[1]

Betsy Caprio

"I'm afraid I'll marry William and I'm afraid I won't," I journaled one night. Those conflicting fears reflected the powerful support I felt from his presence in my life. His generous, loving heart was a safe haven in which I continually took refuge. His devotion undergirded my expanding creativity. Cherished and adored, I continued to grow.

"How my heart melts when I'm with this serene, lovely soul," I acknowledged.

One evening while we were still getting acquainted, I had looked at him over a cup of tea. Unexpectedly I had a rare psychic experience. In my mind's eye a large, ornate book opened before me. I easily read its gold gilt letters: "William was a monk in a Catholic religious order in his last lifetime." Then the book closed.

When I recovered from my surprise, I made so bold as to ask him, "Do you have any sense that you were a monk in a previous lifetime?"

He looked at me with dismay—or was it disgust? There was a long, awkward pause. Finally, "No . . . but a well-recommended psychic once told me that," he begrudgingly admitted.

There was an extraordinary spiritual strength in this man, and a deep spiritual connection between us. "Have we known one another before in a monastic lifetime?" I often pondered. Our tender caring for each other seemed rooted in the very depths of our souls.

Each man who has been important in my life has reflected to me a different part of my own masculine side. From each I have learned something about the hidden richness of myself. William was bringing to me almost a "loving, heavenly Father" quality which I greatly needed at that shaky period of my life. He was truly a gift of God. And, of course, I reflected to William the beauty of his own feminine soul, and he was coming alive in delightful ways before my very eyes.

But, just as each man I've known has developed certain strengths, he's left other areas undeveloped. My surprising peek into William's monk past may have come partly as a warning not to expect proficiency in every area of our relationship.

We'd been dating for several weeks and had shared many tender, passionate kisses. A strong sexual charge was building between us. "How come he isn't whisking me off to a motel," I wondered, "when I've obviously indicated my willingness?" Finally, out of frustration, I requested it!

Then he spoke regretfully of his lack of confidence as a lover. I could see how much he feared disappointing me!

"Well, I'm not that great either," I said, admitting my own insecurities and trying to encourage him.

We were tense and awkward, indeed, when we finally did share sexually. We each seemed to compound the other's fears and rigidities. And after months of "working at" that part of our relationship, even with some professional help, things didn't change much. I began to painfully doubt myself as a woman, and felt his increasing resentment over the impossible task of pleasing me.

I could hardly admit to myself how disappointed I was! I resisted the psychological truth which was now being forced upon me: that a vital, lusty instinctual bond between partners is necessary for full emotional intimacy and the self-healing capacity of a primary relationship. I still tried to persuade myself, "The richness of our other sharing more than compensates for this lack." But my suppressed frustration was accumulating.

Though I continued to have helpful weekly sessions with Prescott, I only skirted this issue. Then one day Prescott pronounced me ready for a woman therapist. Yes, I could feel that maturation in me, too. He referred me to Norinda, under whose warm hands I'd had the mystical return to the Mother.

I respected Norinda as an attractive, "together" woman. In her presence my trust in myself as a woman continued to blossom. One day in her office my frustrations finally exploded.

"I WANT A MAN WHO CAN FUCK ME *MAGNIFICENTLY!*" Then, immediately ashamed of my loud, bold demand upon life, I looked at Norinda timidly. I saw nothing but respect in her eyes.

"Of course you do," she said seriously. "You deserve it. And I'm sure you're going to give that to yourself."

Her words jolted me. They called to mind what I'd learned from my metaphysical studies, "No one can give to us but ourselves, and no one can take away from us but ourselves . . . We inwardly create our outer experiences." I'd been avoiding responsibility for my increasing frustrations, silently blaming William instead. Now I could clearly see that I must leave the security of his sheltering arms and take the next step in "exploring the world and myself in it."

By now I had moved into the privacy of a little cottage. There I created a meditation tape to listen to before I fell asleep each night. I affirmed that I was desirous and *worthy* of a light-hearted, sexy romance with a quality man who would be as enriched by me as I by him. I declared that the universal Mind knew the whereabouts of each of us and was now moving us across the checkerboard of life into one another's embrace. I gave thanks in anticipation of this sweet meeting. I absolutely knew this affirmative prayer technique would work![2]

William and I had been in exclusive relationship for a year and a half. We'd had our ups and downs, but each crisis had produced a deeper level of honest communication and a poignant sense of how dearly we valued each other. We'd both been unwilling, unable, to relinquish the relationship. Now I wept as I told him that I needed to move on to other men. The sadness on his face almost tore me apart. But in the midst of his pain, his spiritual stature was beautifully apparent. He released me with incredible poise and good will, admitting, too, to some relief.

Once he had told me, "This relationship is really rough for me because I realize I'm much more committed to it than you are."

"But there are things I must experience as a single woman," I'd replied. "I cannot consider remarrying for five or maybe ten years."

"Well," he had said, "whatever's right. I'm a very patient man."

Now I felt his generous heart setting me free. But did a thin ray of hope not remain?

38

Sharing The Holy Grail Journey

In Christian language, only by the grace of God can we become whole. Yet, at the same time, a person who would be whole must undergo a great pilgrimage and journey—must search, often painfully, for the ground and fulfillment of his being. It is this mystery of wholeness, which is both the gift of God and the fruit of great effort on the part of man, which is the great theme of the myth of the Holy Grail.[1]

John Sanford

Every part of my life continued to slowly unfold as though by greater design. I still needed a lot of healing solitude in my cottage and my long, meditative walks in nature. Heavy, wracking sobs still frequently overtook me; as I released to them, those storms of emotions served to keep my heart center softened and receptive. Through everything I was steadily learning to trust my deeper self. Time and again I walked to the edge of what light I had, stepped tremulously into the unknowable new and found the next step solidly waiting. When I couldn't proceed from my own intuition, I sought some trusted helper for the guidance I needed to keep my edges growing. Often I marvelled, "So this is the grace of God."

My pastor-friend, John, was one of life's gifts to me. Not only did his prayer group serve as my spiritual support system (and everyone on the transforming journey *must* find a spiritual support system), but he and his wife, Anna, courageously pushed through the resistance of their conservative church board members and invited me to teach adult classes in their Fireside Room. This small flock of sincere seekers was wonderfully responsive to my approach which I described as "a synthesis of depth psychology and the life of the Spirit."

I led a Psychosynthesis[2] series for them, and in teaching this beautiful holistic system of transformation I made its wisdom more truly my own. Next I led a group for women based on Psyche's heroic tale of feminine individuation. I loved creating experiential activities to complement the concepts I taught, and we women were warmed by a profound healing intimacy as we shared the woman's journey around that hearth.

"Helene, you surely plant a powerful seed," one woman summed up as the series ended.

John approached me one day with an extraordinary request. "The women got so much from their class, I'd like you to do a series for men." With a shy smile, he added, "We need it, too."

"But John, men wouldn't come to a men's group led by a woman. And even if they did, they wouldn't be honest in their sharing."

"Well, will you think about it?" he asked earnestly.

I had all but dismissed the idea as preposterous when he asked me again. I gave him more reasons why it wouldn't work.

"I'll help you," he encouraged. "I'll lead the opening meditations if you'll do the rest."

I felt keenly my ignorance of masculine psychology. Had I not just left a marriage in which I felt largely a failure? If I did lead a group, what written resources could I use? I awoke one bright morning knowing intuitively that I *would* be teaching a men's series! I recalled a friend from the past who I was sure could recommend a book for study. But it had been so long; how could I reach him? That very day he called me!

"Stan!" I gasped. "How did you know I needed to talk to you?"

"I just had a feeling to get in touch with you today."

Stan recommended *He*,[3] a Jungian interpretation of the Holy Grail story. It was exactly the book we needed.

The old cliché about the teacher learning the most applied to me as I created the eight-week series. Since my divorce I'd been so preoccupied with licking my male-related wounds, I'd had little energy for tackling the male viewpoint. The book's forward was written by a woman psychologist, and she forced me to begin to look:

> *Women often labor under the delusion that life is really pretty easy for men, at least when compared to their own lot, and have no idea what a complicated struggle is really involved in the transition from male childhood to real manhood. They have no idea of the long and arduous road which must be travelled by the male child who must separate himself from the original, indispensable, nurturing mother and venture forth into a way of experiencing himself which is not her way, and which he cannot learn from her, either by example or by instruction . . . A boy must learn to be different from her without this difference deteriorating into either antagonism or fear.*[4]

As I pondered this, it fell into place beside John Sanford's lecture which had taught me so much:

> *Men tend to see women as though they are all the same. While he remains at a very unconscious level—which is where most men are—he tends to see women either as mother, or, unconsciously as an extension of himself. Or, he sees her as filling his need for pleasurable gratification, which is another way of saying he sees her as mother . . . Now that's one of the things you're up against as women.*

As I continued to study, an insight from *The Hazards of Being Male* brought this all into focus for me. I was sobered as I read:

> *. . . the male who thinks he's found an earth-mother will only get hooked into relating to her regressively—aborting his own growth and being much less of a human being than he is potentially.*[5]

I could see that only a rare man completes that long and arduous journey from male childhood to the full power of manhood. My smoldering residue of anger was now mitigated by sadness—sadness for the men who don't make it to maturity. And yes—I admit it—I felt sad for us women who've had them for fathers and for mates. I was struck by the tragedy of injured daughters who grow up to marry injured men, who together spawn more injured sons and daughters, passing the curse through countless generations.

I was inundated by painful memories from my personal legacy of that collective tragedy. As I prepared the series, I had no choice but to accelerate my inner prayer work toward releasing, forgiving the past. That discipline, plus a lot of new understanding, brought greater compassion to my softening, opening heart.

39

Empowering My Son's Journey

. . . inner wholeness seems to attract, in magnet fashion, outer situations that reflect it. Thus we find that women who are carriers of both the feminine and the masculine energies in harmony having doors "miraculously" opened for them in the outer world, doors that give them opportunities for the sort of equality other women have gone to the barricades for—and failed to achieve.[1]

Betsy Caprio

My cozy cottage became an ideal incubation chamber for my expanding inner life. Here, I faithfully continued to build a whole new sense of my own identity. From the level of my will, I'd obviously said "Yes!" to a major overhaul.

Each morning I propped myself up in bed for a bit of inspirational reading followed by my quiet period of transcendental meditation. Then I concluded with some strong affirmations either spoken or chanted aloud with considerable power. For instance: *"I AM daughter of the One Creative Life of God, made in Its image and likeness. I now express the Infinite's boundless creativity and transforming love everywhere in my world. Because I am one with God, all things are now possible in my life."* My little house seemed almost to smile in response to these enthusiastic declarations of truth![2]

Finding my own place to live had corresponded to my further growth toward autonomy, independence.

"Whenever I drag my feet regarding the next growing step, life provides me with a swift kick in the right direction," I noted wryly in my journal. I had lived with my widow-friend for a year; she was a kind, generous woman, so that had been a happy arrangement until I unwisely confided to her that my relationship to William included sex. She expressed the shock I should have expected from her traditional religious stance. She, in fact, was lonely for a man in her life, and even though she was not letting that need be filled, I sensed some jealousy of my social life. She asked me to leave!

That shook me up, but I soon realized that the timing was perfect. I lifted in prayer my urgent need for a new home—and lifted it and lifted it—till I felt an inner assurance that "All is in order." Then I relaxed, and a series of blessed "coincidences" led me to the cottage the day before it was to be advertised in the paper.

My new landlady was also an older widow, but this time she lived in the big house next door. She had no interest in my lifestyle.

This was my first experience ever of living by myself. For a couple weeks I felt terribly lonely and at sea. I cried a lot and also got a very bad cold. The cottage felt strange, as though it contained the atmosphere of the previous occupants, so I played my favorite classical music by the hour to change the ambience. It worked; within a few weeks I felt real contentment in my own space.

I was still helping carpool Rolf to his alternative school in the mountains. I treasured these opportunities to be with this quiet, introverted son who'd grown into a willowy six-footer. Now I felt free to bring him home with me after school to share over a snack. The thing Michael had predicted came beautifully to fruition: "As you get more honest about your own feelings, more flowing, more in contact with yourself, you'll find a rich relationship developing with that child. But don't go looking for it. . . . He'll just respond to you when you're in that place. He can't help but open up to you."

Rolf and I now discovered a deep, almost wordless communion. I was able to give him the loving support he needed as he courageously gathered his strength to leave home. He was only sixteen and so vulnerable. "He's been forced to grow up too fast," I realized sadly. But I could feel the rightness of his decision, for he wanted to try his fledgling wings in the east near his sister and her circle of energetic young friends. And he absolutely knew he could not be a part of the new family his Dad was creating.

Rolf confided to his few friends at school, "Sometimes I'm so lonely. My Mom is the only one I have to talk to."

My heart almost exploded with joy over the privilege of being Rolf's trusted friend. My new awareness of the man's difficult journey made me very tender toward this precious son. But it was the strength accruing from my own hard-won steps toward freedom that now equipped me to empower his.

40

"You'll Always Have Men In Your Life"

*. . . the new opportunity came at the exact moment of
readiness. The synchronicity is impressive; always
it is manifest when the spirit is truly at work.*[1]

Helen M. Luke

Norinda gasped in astonishment when I told her, "I'm going to
lead a series for men—and nine have already paid in full."

Then her face dissolved into a knowing smile. "Helene, you'll
always have men in your life."

I happily called Michael to tell him about the group. "It'll do
you worlds of good!" he exclaimed.

Indeed, the series served my need to grow as much as it served
those good men who gathered with me around the hearth. And
I'm pleased to tell you that they reported practical benefits from
it.

"My husband is getting an awful lot from your group," one wife
called me to say. Her husband amplified, "Since our last session
I finally understand what she's been asking from me in important
interactions between us."

Obviously the Spirit of truth was at work in spite of my new
relationship to the subject. I enjoyed creating guided imagery and
dyadic exercises from the Holy Grail material. In addition, I
brought in some holistic experiences from Aikido and bioener-
getics. For two of the eight evenings I invited guest leaders whom
I admired as men. John provided ongoing spiritual leadership in
a beautiful way.

The group had an unexpected value for me which I now delight
in sharing with you!

Dan had signed up eagerly at the very first announcement. He
was tall, handsome, in his early forties, divorced. He always came
in carrying his motorcycle helmet under his arm. "May I give you
a ride sometime?" he smiled down at me.

Perhaps it was my fear of motorcycles that delayed my recognition of the sweetness he'd be bringing to my life. (I was still
using my affirmation for a new love affair.) About the time the
series ended I finally wised up. I called Dan one evening, took a
deep breath and said:

"YES!"

41

Motorcycle Mama

To be ever conscious of the possible hazards before
us snatches away our power to leap. We can only live
fully by risking our lives over and over again . . . Is
it not a fact that the people who accept death most
readily are the ones who have lived most fully?[1]
Irene Claremont de Castillejo

When our son, Clark, was a college freshman he'd asked us for
money to buy a motorcycle.

"No way!" Len and I had chorused. "Do you think we've invested
eighteen years in raising you to help you go out and kill yourself?"

I squirmed recalling that conversation the day I first donned
a helmet and awkwardly climbed on the back of Dan's powerful
Moto Guzzi. As we sped rapidly away I clung to him for dear life
and literally prayed without ceasing! On the second ride I relaxed
enough to experience the wonder of trees arching high over our
heads as we sped smoothly along. Travelling a road through a
towering redwood forest—without the usual enclosing cubicle of
steel and glass—is pure magic! Especially with your body pressed
close and your arms wrapped around a man you're loving.

This romance was made to order. Dan was also in a freedom-
loving, exploration period in his life. He was charming, sensitive,
easy going. And he'd become very adept at expressing his sexuality.

I admired his obvious enjoyment of living in his body. I'd never
found "embodiment" that easy. But in partnership with him, I
found touching, cuddling, making love most natural and delightful. I'd often lie awake beside him as he slept just to feel his
strong, hot masculine energy. How it fed me! My heart opened
tenderly and passionately to this dear man, and we were both
warmed by that energizing flow.

He told me admiringly, "I feel like top banana having *you* for
my girl friend." Seemingly unbothered by the fact that I was five
years older than he, Dan enthused, "There's a freshness about
you I just love."

We explored much of California's extraordinary beauty together, often travelling with a motorcycle club to the mountains
or seashore. What a revelation to find friendly, middle-aged cou-
ples in the club instead of Hell's Angels!

Eventually I took my courage in hand and wrote my children about my adventures. With a wry smile I signed my letters, "Motorcycle Mama." They were amazed but very tactful, I noted.

Clark then felt an implied permission to belatedly purchase his own two wheels. He did; but by this time he was in medical school and was seeing many serious traffic-related injuries. His enthusiasm waned, and his second-hand Honda finally rusted away.

Lynn had married in the east and had her first child. Rolf was now living in a studio apartment near her and working for her husband. I occasionally signed my letters to them, "Motorcycle Grandma."

My children had all along celebrated my increasing aliveness. In fact, they were supportive of both their Dad and me, seeing how life had improved for us both since our divorce.

But this Helene Joy—was she not an enigma to them? Was this Aphrodite on wheels their formerly rigid and uptight Mom? She was suddenly younger, relishing the sweetness of romance and adventure. Where would her awakening take her next?

42

Soft, Yet Assertive

Her urge to assert herself struck at the heart of her Christian ideals. Her analysis . . . led to a major reinterpretation of her faith. . . . Genuine devotion to God presupposes an authentic ego identity, developed as a result of full contact with life . . .[1]

Ann Belford Ulanov

The same ego which, when centered on itself, defensively leads to neurosis, also leads toward growth when it centers on something larger and more all-inclusive than itself. . . . The essential ego [is] rooted in the Self.[2]

Elizabeth B. Howes & Sheila Moon

With Dan I found myself practicing new ways to relate. Norinda helped spark my expansion in this area.

I told her, "My pattern has always been to take care of the men in my life, to mother them. That has been true even when I also sought fathering from them."

"Yes, and as women get older they often think the only way they can get a man is to take care of him," Norinda offered. "But a healthier attitude is, 'I'm strong; I'm assertive; and I take care of myself first.' "

"I'm feeling myself more in that place now."

"I know you are. And while you've been doing that you've been getting younger and softer. You're much less matronly than when you first came to see me. The girl in you is coming out." That was delightfully apparent to me as I compared photographs of myself. I'd dropped eight to ten years since my divorce.

One day Dan wanted me to do something with him, and I found myself saying, "I don't feel like it."

"How come?" he asked, surprised.

"I just don't feel like it." I surprised myself! Since my response was not angry or defensive, he accepted it without feeling diminished.

I loved it when Norinda shared with me out of her own experience as a woman. "Softness and the ability to assert go hand in hand. How could I dare be soft and yielding if I didn't have the strength to protect that? Backed up by my strength, I can be vulnerable and really allow myself to be touched."

I confided to her something that had bothered me for such a long time. "Sometimes I'm scared because I have so much more strength than the men in my life. So I squelch a part of myself."

"Yes, and then you attract men out of your incompleteness—the kind who can handle other parts of you but not your strength. You'll have to be *all* of yourself out there in the world in order to attract the kind of men you really want." She continued, "When you're working here with your anger and your rage, your whole body gets involved, and you're so alive, so beautiful, so full of 'oom-pah'. And you're very sexy!"

I sighed deeply. "I've always yearned for a man who'll look me straight in the eye and say, *'Lady, you've met your match!'* "

"Sure you have. So be your whole self out there and attract a man who can handle your 'oom-pah.' "

Accepting my own power would be an ongoing challenge. For as long as I could remember I had feared that power, for it had typically come roaring forth when driven by my harsh, negative animus. But that was changing. I was well along toward a positive relationship between my now more helpful animus and my female self. That basic change affected everything in my life. One night I wept with a heart full of gratitude as I recognized my progress in these words:

> *Through this redeemed animus the woman gains a relation to the masculine principle within herself... the Logos ... wisdom.... Thus ... is born a new spiritual power transforming the life of the individual.*[3]

"How has this remarkable change occurred?" I journaled through my thankful tears. "Only by degrees," I realized, "by faithfully choosing to let suffering shatter me and soften my heart. And by my deep commitment to wholeness and to the Highest Plan for my life." Now my new understanding helped explain the former negativity of my animus-power:

> *If the woman does not help her animus, he goes off and creates mischief. He must have his chance to live.*[4]
> *It is when purpose is lacking that the masculine in a woman becomes negative.*[5]

I'd come a long way since those frustrating years of unsuccessfully (and resentfully) trying to be the "good daughter," then the "good wife" behind the husband, suppressing so much of my essential self in the process. No wonder my creative animus power had turned toxic, threatening, explosive! This part of me needed to live, to express, to genuinely serve in the world.

I was learning from Norinda that a woman can be at once powerful and emotionally beautiful. She'd developed her own strong mind, enabling her to think independently, to make conscious choices, to work with integrity toward her goals. Yet she'd not broken faith with her instinctive womanhood.

One night I exulted in my journal, "Praise the Lord! I see that I can be soft *and* strong *and* sexual *and* spiritual." I knew this balanced wholeness was possible for I beheld Norinda demonstrating it.

43

Wounded Healer

If a person has gone through a crisis, died to an old
personality, and fought his or her way back to health
and a more conscious life, that person may gain a
certain quality that enables him to put others in touch
with healing, too.[1]

John Sanford

I continued to grow professionally as well as personally. I'd
been promised earlier, "Just be about the Father-Mother's business. Trust that you'll be guided one step at a time."

Now I was obedient to a strong pull toward serious training in
massage. I committed myself to an intensive several-month course
which gave me California state certification in wholistic massage.
Truly, I loved it! We were taught both oriental and western techniques for releasing energy blocks in the human system. The
training honored the body-mind-spirit relationship I had intuitively recognized for many years. And it acknowledged the power
of nurturing touch as a bona fide healing art. How well I remembered my own peak experience of returning to the Mother under
Norinda's skillful, caring hands!

Gradually, I evolved my own bodywork therapy approach by
synthesizing massage healing techniques with my counseling
skills. It proved amazingly effective in many cases where insight
therapy alone would have failed. And it served my own deep need
to touch lives in a healing, transforming way.

Her conviction that she is a light-bearer, God-carrier,
will give her life purpose . . . This sort of "spiritual
maternity" may come more easily to women because
of their capacity for physical maternity (whether or
not the latter is ever realized).[2]

44

Fireworks In My Head

When the student is ready, the teacher will [re] appear.

Eastern teaching

Dan suggested one day, "Let's get a house together."

I was no longer opposed on moral grounds to the idea of living with a man outside of marriage. When both Clark and Lynn had embraced that lifestyle I'd worked through to an acceptance of it as a healthy alternative to premature marriage, especially for young people. After my divorce I'd only gradually decided it would be all right for me, too. (Later, I wondered if I'd ever marry a man I hadn't lived with first.)

But I lacked enthusiasm for Dan's suggestion even though he was bringing a lot of succulence into my life. I noticed he'd often shy away from a close psychological intimacy when I tried to initiate that deep kind of sharing, and this disappointed me. Also, the freedom I'd found living alone had become so very precious.

I did sense that my relationship to Dan had reached a turning point. It was a living thing which could only continue to grow toward greater intimacy or begin to die. "Which way?" I wondered with some concern.

Other compelling things were on my mind. I was planning my third annual summer trip to Virginia Beach, Virginia to visit my children. During my previous summer's visit, I'd acted upon a friend's suggestion and asked for an interview at the Association for Research and Enlightenment (the Edgar Cayce organization) there. I'd felt immediate rapport with their fine staff, and was invited to teach my class for "Women in Transition and Transformation" at one of their conferences the following summer.

Now the time was fast approaching, and every time I thought ahead to that week at the A.R.E., a joyous burst of light filled my head like fireworks. What was in store? It was my first opportunity to gain some national visibility for my work. But the strong energy burst suggested an even greater significance.

I told Dan I wouldn't be making any important decisions until I returned from the east; he was understanding.

A few days before my trip my phone woke me with its urgent ringing early one morning.

"Helene, this is Michael. I'm vacationing in California. Would you like to see me?" (He had moved to Colorado a year before.)

"Yes, I would!" I exclaimed with gratitude. "Today!"

45

"Stay On Your Path"

While human nature resists change, spiritual unfoldment compels change, breaking up the old patterns continuously.[1]

Joel Goldsmith

Michael and I were so happy to see each other! As we embraced with tender affection, I noticed what a fine, mature man he'd become, full of solid spiritual authority. I prepared tea, and we soon got down to business as I sought his counsel for this next turning point in my life.

"You've made some radical changes!" he exclaimed with a frank look of admiration. That was the most validation I'd ever felt from him. His quick perception of my hard-won growth greatly pleased me.

"Well," he continued, "I see that your place of power has now moved to the east coast. Can't you feel that?"

"I can feel change ahead, for sure."

"Well, there's work for you back there, an incredible opportunity to make a fresh start where people have no images of you based on your past; you'd find them relating to you with a respect you've never had . . . .I see some opportunity opening up, a metaphysical school of some sort, where you'll do bodywork and teaching—work on a multi-dimensional level. You can make a real contribution there." I told him about my upcoming week at the A.R.E. conference, and wondered if he were seeing that. "I don't know if what I'm looking at is the A.R.E. or not. But the fireworks in your head are not because of just *one week's* work in the east!"

He went on with rising enthusiasm. "I see travel back there, too. You're going to put together your own workshops based on what has been meaningful in your life over the past several years. You'll find that you're a very powerful teacher."

"I'd have to leave a sweet relationship with a man," I said wistfully.

As always, Michael was totally honest and confronting. "Helene, I can see that you're growing at a much faster rate than this man in terms of autonomy and inner strength. There's a dimension of maturity you've moved into that you haven't connected with yet in a relationship. You're still settling for less. Now, if you do move back east you may be on your own for awhile till you stabilize in a new reality pattern. But in about a year I see a level of relating to men open up beyond anything you've ever had. See, everything's been a progression, and you're ready for the next big step." He paused thoughtfully, then added with emphasis, "Yep, it will be a *powerful* relationship."

"OH GOD," I moaned loudly, both thrilled and terrified at the prospect.

Michael dropped his serious demeanor and heartily laughed at me! Then he continued, "This love affair with Dan has been important; it has given you tremendous validation as a woman. But you'd come to regret it if you stayed here because of a man. *Don't commit yourself to anything except staying on your own Path, to following your own sense of where you feel most vital and alive.*" I felt firm confirmation of that from within even as he spoke.

He summed up modestly, "All this I've told you may be off the wall. So just file it away, and if it seems to be checking out, go for it . . . But I feel like your west coast time is done for now. I see you in the east for one to three years."

"Wow!" I had a strong conviction that what he saw was *not* off the wall. Once again I felt like he'd read the higher blueprint of my life, had delivered to me the next set of instructions from my guiding Self. Though I questioned him some about the things he'd said, mostly I just kept saying "Wow!"

That was the last time I saw my beautiful mentor, Michael. He returned to Colorado and dropped from my sight. I attempted once to find a phone listing for him in the intervening years, unsuccessfully.

Michael had always explained his life's purpose as that of "a servant of the Universe." At several strategic junctures he'd been present to me as a true prophet of God, powerfully launching me upon my new Way. I am humbled to contemplate such a profound gift of grace. And I know for a certainty that to each person who sincerely embraces the rigors of the transforming Journey, God's Way-showers—both seen and unseen—are faithfully sent.

46

Leaving Dead, Dry Bones

It begins with an assent. A woman says "yes" to something that is going to change her whole life and the lives of others. . . . An invitation is heard and . . . accepted. Thereafter we are not our own, nor on our own. We are given and anything can happen.[1]

Rosemary Haughton

. . . real freedom from servitude comes . . . through the choice of another binding commitment. We may do what we will only when we have learned the nature of love.[2]

Helen M. Luke

My class for the conference women in Virginia Beach was received with such enthusiasm that I was asked to repeat it a few days later for the A.R.E. staff-women. I did so, and indeed experienced myself as a powerful teacher as I shared authentically from my own emerging personhood. It was very exciting!

However, my inquiries revealed that there were no regular staff openings in their organization. So I returned from my vacation without knowing what it was Michael had clairvoyantly seen.

Dan met me at the airport, and as we arrived at the little cottage I'd loved so well, I found myself saying, "This place feels like a pile of dead, dry bones. What am I doing here?"

Truly, I had left all the "juice" behind in the east. That much of Michael's prediction was certainly checking out. But I settled back in again, glad to rest from my trip in the familiarity of home.

Not for long! Within a few days I got a strong impulse to start cleaning out my closets. Even while my hands were obedient to that task, my fearful self occasionally resisted its obvious implications. "Dear God, am I really to cast free again? I'm a *woman*. Am I never to know a secure nest on this earth?"

I struggled to find the faith I needed. One prayerful night it finally came. "O.K.!" I joyously assented. "Lead on! My heart is ready to trust You for the next leg of the Journey." Then a weight lifted and I was seized by an incredible energy burst radiating from my chest into my entire being.

*Some force beyond her knowing had entered and pos-
sessed her . . . and she knew, in a way beyond conscious knowing, that the seed of the spirit had entered
into her and that, as soul, she had conceived.*[3]

This was not the first time I had exulted in a powerful invasion
of that impregnating Light! It had first happened much earlier
in my journey—a decade before—but now my spiritual rheostat
was definitely, dramatically turned up again.

So I discarded fully half my clothes, and, still buoyed up by the
blessed warmth of that inner current, I began happily culling the
rest of my meager household furnishings. But as more days went
by, fear crept in again for I still had no hint of where I'd be going.
I was dismantling my only home, preparing to step off into an
unknown void.

One day I dug in my heels like a balky mule. "Hey, my financial
resources are limited, and at my age I lack sufficient stamina to
rebuild my life from scratch. There's not one more thing going
out of this house till I'm told where I'm going!"

With that decision the glorious energy suddenly dammed up
inside me. I felt like an explosion just waiting to happen. Frant-
ically, I rushed over to see an intuitive woman friend for help.

"You'll have to get back into cooperation with that flow or blow
apart," she cautioned. She was telling me what I already knew!
I'd chosen to take the next step on the journey and it wasn't going
to work to turn back now. Then my friend added, "By the way,
when I was back east I visited a wonderful Quaker study-com-
munity near Philadelphia. It's a place for learning and contem-
plation, and an opportunity to experience living in a spiritual
community. I really feel guided to suggest you look into it."

This was my first clue! Even as I resumed clearing out my
house—and the inner current immediately resumed its buoyant
flow—I wasted no time in finding out about Pendle Hill. First I
asked my pastor-friend, John, if he knew of it.

"Oh yes! Pendle Hill is renowned as a balance point in American
religious tradition, where cultivation of the inner life is wed to
effective service to the world. They do some significant publishing
there. I'm thrilled to think you're inquiring about it."

The Pendle Hill catalog[4] revealed a permanent staff of thirty-
five people and another thirty-five residential students who come
in for each academic year. The students are typically aged nineteen to seventy-five, from diverse religious backgrounds, often at
turning points in their personal or professional lives. A student

can take non-credit classes there or do independent study, and participate in the spiritual life of the community as much as desired. Each day begins with a silent "Meeting for Worship" in the fine Quaker tradition of attuning to the inner Light. Students and staff alike share the daily chores. As I eagerly read, an inner quickening convinced me that this was my place!

But they were already full for the upcoming year, and the best they could do was put me on a waiting list. They gave me no encouragement. And their fall term would begin in just seven weeks.

Still, I had an absolute conviction by now that I was soon moving east. And I couldn't shake the feeling that my destination was Pendle Hill. Incredible as it seems, I continued emptying my house, selling or giving away the rest of my possessions.

One day I wrote in my journal, "I know I'm going east even if I have to initially get a job scrubbing floors!" I gave my landlady notice. My own conviction impressed me.

I wrote back to Pendle Hill and told them, "I am moving east, though I don't yet know where. I can be reached at my California address till Sept. ninth. After that . . . I'll have to get in touch with you."

The feeling that I was going to Pendle Hill persisted. I found myself paradoxically resting in the deep calm of that uncanny assurance even while fretting with an unsettling surface tension. How long would it take them to also recognize that I belonged there? Or would they?

47

"Are You Ready For Helene Joy?"

The feminine way . . . is to wait until something gives her the means and the way and the courage . . . A man can [also] do this by acting out of his feminine side. It is a divine giving up . . . a getting back to a very still inner center . . . this is a creative act . . . She is receptive, not passive.[1]

Robert Johnson

As I prayerfully held to the conviction that my Highest Good was working out, my application for admission was causing a little flurry at Pendle Hill, I later learned. I must have sounded awfully eager! They were intrigued, too, with my resumé, with my eclectic training and wholistic work. John wrote a strong letter of recommendation for me, but my most important recommendation came from a member of their own board of directors, a beautiful Quaker woman I'd met through my daughter in Virginia Beach. I'd shared with her some of my insights gained as a non-traditional counselor in California.

"Is Helene Joy ready for a year of living in spiritual community here at Pendle Hill?" the admissions office finally phoned her to ask.

"Yes, Helene Joy is ready for Pendle Hill. But the question you should be asking is this: 'Is Pendle Hill ready for Helene Joy?' "

My phone rang cheerily one morning in late August. "We've created a place for you in our student body. We're looking forward to having you here." Oh, thank you, God; you've parted the Red Sea before me again.

I began tying up loose ends, seeing my few clients for the last time and referring them to colleagues.

I wrote a farewell letter to the many people I'd worked with through the years, most of whom still associated me with my years as Len's wife. "I'm on my way!" I exulted. "This long chapter of living, dying, soaring, and serving is now complete. I leave California with tremendous gratitude to so many of you. We've all been teachers helping one another grow."

As I prepared to leave the humble cottage which had sheltered me so well, I gave it my thankful blessing. I was deeply moved to feel my kinship with this poetic wisdom:

And alone and without his nest shall the eagle fly across the sun.[2]

48

Magical, Mystical Bliss

I do not believe anyone ever learned to love. Love happens. It is a miracle that happens by grace . . . It comes, it lights our lives, and very often it departs. We can never make it happen 'nor make it stay.[1]
Irene Claremont de Castillejo

Dan was keenly disappointed, yet gracious about my plans to move away. "I see you're at a point in your life where you can't yet make a commitment. But you'll come back someday," he said hopefully.

As it happened, there were sufficient days remaining for us to take the vacation trip he'd earlier proposed—on his motorcycle, of course. That trip proved to be the exclamation point capping our lovely season as sweethearts.

Pulling a small trailer with camping gear behind the motorcycle, we set off for an eight-day adventure through the fabled scenery of the Pacific northwest, all the way up to British Columbia. It was wonderful new territory to me. Each day we rode for several hours, but I've almost forgotten the aches and shakes of a week on an iron steed. Truly, what I recall is the sheer magic of those days.

What were the ingredients of that magic? Primarily, the nourishing masculine-feminine energy field we created as our bodies pressed close together hour after hour in loving, relaxed harmony. It was by far the greatest bliss I'd ever sustained over an extended period of time. We were happy, carefree lovers, living in the moment, relishing the beauty of the earth and one another. So close was our attunement, when I'd literally weep over the majesty of redwood forests, deep river canyons, and crashing ocean surf, Dan would feel me quietly weeping and reach back to squeeze my knee. And the evening we saw thousands of glistening gulls stretching to infinity against a rainbow's vivid hues, did he share my mystical experience of seeing other realities, of skies *above* skies? In his own way I'm sure he did. We became as one during those magical, mystical days.

Energized by our personal closeness, I was often lifted to a sense of transpersonal oneness with all life. As my joy bubbled up and spilled over, that motorcycle became a moving "power point" from which prayer went winging forth across the land. And I felt the earth gratefully receiving those blessings from my flowing heart.

Perhaps that trip with Dan was the high culmination of my carefree adolescence. Was it a joyous rite of passage? There would be other times of man-woman bliss ahead. But for that whole week I knew the sweet abandonment of my feminine spirit to tenderness and beauty. I truly wondered, "Is this not my watershed experience in this lifetime upon the earth?"

49

Hippie Heroine

She has emerged from her incubation container. And
she must have asked, as so many of her sisters emerg-
ing from homes and sheltering parents and outgrown
jobs and completed relationships throughout history
have asked, "Can I make it on my own?"[1]

Betsy Caprio

The day came for my departure to the east coast. It was the
ending of an era, the beginning of the new.

It was William who helped me load my car. He and I had evolved
a beautiful soul brother-sister relationship during those months
of my romance with Dan. William had more than demonstrated
that his devoted love for me transcended everything.

He was inspired by my willingness to pull up stakes and strike
out alone. For he'd known me, had been my mainstay during the
shakiest, weepiest, stretchingest period of my new life. He'd con-
sistently cheered my growth, and courageously transcended any
desire he may have felt to possess me.

But now as we packed the car, he could not entirely conceal his
grieving. We both knew that I might never come back.

We loaded my old station wagon to the gills, even tying my
bicycle on the top. I smile to remember that my car fit the ster-
eotype of a California hippie's—and here I was going to the conservative east! ("Are you ready for Helene Joy?")

That old Chevrolet became an integral part of my heroine's
journey, so I must give it honorable mention. Len and I and our
young children had named it "The Blue Angel" when we bought
it new in 1964, sparkling metallic blue with regal white top and
gleaming chrome. But by the time it became mine in the divorce
settlement, it had served us for over a decade and more than
100,000 miles. Two of our teenagers had learned to drive in it.
By now its paint was chipped and faded and some of its chrome
was missing. And what a lot of memories it contained! It still ran
well and frequently elicited the praise of mechanics who serviced
it. "That was the best engine GM ever made," they encouraged
me.

That car became for me a symbol of my own undaunted spirit.
For I, also, had been scarred by life, yet had endured. And like

the Blue Angel's quality V-8 engine, I still had the power to go where my destiny called me.

Now it would transport everything I owned, for I'd kept only what I felt I absolutely could not do without. It held my clothes for all seasons, including the thermal underwear and cheerful, red wool coat I'd bought for east coast winters. (Was I glad!) It held the precious, carefully-selected books I would use for independent study at Pendle Hill, a lot of them by insightful women authors of Jungian viewpoint. It held the tools of my trade—my folding massage table, music-therapy cassettes and tape player. And, of course, my indispensable bicycle and some indoor exercise equipment on the top.

Side by side, William and I worked till the loading was complete. Then we looked at each other, and lengthily, quietly embraced.

As I drove slowly away, he stood straight and solemn in heartfelt salute. I was strengthened by the deep respect I saw in his eyes.

50

Goodbye, Dad

If the relationship with the father has been impaired, it is important for the woman to understand the wound, to appreciate what has been lacking so that it can be developed within.[1]

Linda Leonard

My first stop was but two hours away, for I wanted to see my father before I left California. I sensed it might be our last visit, though he was in apparently excellent health and enjoying his devoted new wife.

I found Dad worrying about me. He did not share my faith that my old car could make such a long trip, and most assuredly did not understand the whole symbolic significance of this, my spiritual journey. Though he didn't say so, I think he was dismayed that I'd not married William whom he'd found to be "a prince of a man."

Yet, Dad helped me by making sure I had my route mapped out and by buying me a tarp to cover the things on my luggage rack. As I watched his skillful hands tie it on securely, I felt great nostalgia. I realized that he was supporting me in the only way he knew—as he always had—and love was beneath the surface of his dour manner.

My sadness was mingled with relief as I finally kissed him goodbye. I inwardly lifted Dad up to God as I started on my journey. But my release of him was not complete; there was much more ahead to do.

As spring blossomed at Pendle Hill, my premonition of his impending death grew stronger. I took many solitary walks along the creek that meandered through beautiful woods near the campus. There I entered into mourning for my father.

Instead of the hurt, resentful feelings I typically had when I thought of him, I began spontaneously recalling little scenes from my childhood when he *was* there for me. I saw him teaching me to ride my bike, and saw his skillful hands crafting me a fine chest of drawers for my twelfth Christmas. I recalled sitting by my Daddy in church, watching him reverently bow his head in prayer. Even as a very little girl I sensed in him an admirable spiritual force. I felt the strength of his integrity, of his sincere yearning for a Christ-filled life. How I loved and adored him then! How proud I was as the church people flocked to his weekly Bible class! As these nourishing memories poured forth I often wept aloud with only the trees to witness my melting heart.

At the same time, my hours of study forced me to confront his inevitable deficiencies as a father. He was emotionally a fearful man, often caught in a negative expression of his natural spiritual force. His marriage to Mom had been fraught with clutching and conflict like Len's and mine. How this limited them—and us—as parents!

In my studies I found sobering insights about our father-daughter relationship. For instance:

> . . . *animus possession in a woman is especially ir-*
> *ritating for a man. . . . When a girl begins to have*
> *her own ideas . . . the father hears his daughter and*
> *feels the animus growing, and having disliked and*
> *loathed that in his wife and in other women . . . he*
> *comes down on it. It is an age-old tragedy that the*
> *beginnings of mental activities in the daughters are*
> *smashed or doomed by the father's reaction. Many*
> *women are seriously lamed on the mental and spir-*
> *itual side, and in their work, because the father, in*
> *a bad moment, had told them they could not do some-*

> *thing. . . . The creative animus is so sensitive at that*
> *stage that one cannot regain one's enthusiasm.*[2]

It was ironic, I thought bitterly, that Dad had backed up his students so well. As Superintendent of Schools in our small Minnesota town, he was tireless in helping his brightest young graduates obtain scholarships for higher education. Long after he retired, his Christmas mail still held appreciative notes from former students who'd made good.

But at home his insecure, critical self was so manifest. Dad was wounded, both in relationship to his own feminine side, and in his masculinity. I wept to realize that if Dad had succeeded in owning his power as a man, he wouldn't have felt threatened by my growing strength. And I would have had a positive model instead of a judging, haranguing one, for my developing animus.

> *For a woman to find the masculine within her and*
> *establish a relationship to it, she dearly needs at least*
> *one fine human model of what is manly, in an evolved*
> *form.*[3]

More painful insights surfaced. In *The Wounded Woman: Healing the Father-Daughter Relationship,*[4] Linda Leonard describes how a woman with inadequate fathering typically becomes either an "armored Amazon" (rigid, controlling, cut-off from her own feminine flow), or the "eternal girl" who falls into the despair of weakness and relates to life as a helpless victim. And the same woman, at different times, may live out both. I recognized myself! Now I understood the baffling paradox of my "Proud Lady" and "Miss Pitiful." Both adaptations separated me from my real self and had caused me great suffering. The author gave hope to women thus fragmented, drawn from her own courageous journey, but didn't gloss over the high cost of such inner healing.

"But I've already come a long way," I realized. Much of my "Proud Lady" armoring had shattered during the last painful period with Len. (Nan had seen it as the mannequin sliced open to release the real woman curled up inside.) And I'd been forced to find my inner springs of feminine spiritual strength in order to survive, thus dispelling the worst of my "helpless victim" propensity.

But heartache lingered as I grieved over years and years bereft of love. At what cost I had armored my heart! "How could I possibly have succeeded in any intimate relationship?" I honestly confronted.

She saw, in this illumined moment, that the depth-dark failure of her marriage was that it had confirmed both her childhood distrust of her own power to give or to inspire love, and her doubt of the integrity and loyalty or the hidden motive of the person who offered it. Distrust had permeated every form of relatedness: love, friendship, profession, and had even distorted her image of God. Bereft of trust she had drawn a circle of isolation about herself, all the time telling herself it was others—even the inward Other—who shut her from life.[5]

"HOW CAN I EVER MAKE PEACE WITH THIS FATHERING DEFICIENCY?" I raged from my woundedness. "I can't afford this poisonous resentment!"

As if in answer, the Pendle Hill bookstore introduced me to a remarkable author, Helen M. Luke. I would later travel to Michigan to meet this wise woman personally, such was the impact of her writing upon my spirit. Her inspiring words on the symbolism of "Rumplestiltskin" helped me finally take responsibility for choosing this man as my father.

As you remember, the tale begins with a poor peasant boasting that his daughter can spin straw into gold. This boast reaches the King with life-threatening consequences for the seemingly unfortunate girl.

Fairy stories almost always have this character of "all or nothing"—reflecting a basic truth of the psyche. . . . In the imagery of the story, either we must turn the straw of our lives into gold, in which case we will marry the King, that is, find the royal creative meaning of our lives and bring forth our "child"; or, if we fail to do so, we will lose our heads, lose all possibility of coming to individual consciousness.

We should think for a moment about the father's role in getting his daughter into this pickle. We are all very ready to go back and lay the blame for our troubles on our parents' blindness—and to recognize their mistakes is usually an essential step along the way. But, as we look deeper, we see that it is precisely to these mistakes that we owe the stimulus which forces us to seek the truth in our own way, if we will pay the price. The girl's father does a terrible thing

to her because of his selfish pride. His guilt remains,
but for her it is, we may imagine, the only thing which
could have forced her to face the basic "either-or" and
so launched her on her own unique and "royal" way.[6]

Dad came to me in a dream one memorable night that year. He waved a loving, smiling goodbye before disappearing over the crest of a hill. My heart was pierced by his sweetness, his inherent goodness. I awoke sobbing, filled with an unspeakable sense of loss. But when the storm of emotion passed, the peace of acceptance took its place.

Only a few weeks later the call came. A heart attack had taken Dad quickly into the next life.

51

"Like A Pearl, It Has A Price"

Thus she enters on the quest for her true identity as
an individual woman. The way will bring her into
darkness and loneliness, through fire and water, but
at the last she will begin to discover that unpossessive
love between persons which brings renewal of faith
in life itself and finally the 'agape' of wholeness.[1]

Helen M. Luke

"I know what I'm here to study," I told the dean at Pendle Hill, showing him my books. "I'm involved in a deep personal research project concerning what it is to be a woman. This is the strongest impetus of my life."

I recalled how Michael had once told me, "It will take you several more years of heavy work. It's bigger than most would choose to take on. Like a pearl, it has a price."

"I wish all our students were as clear about what they're here for," the dean said graciously.

Pendle Hill was a wholesome place to keep my edges growing. All aspects of the community reflected the Quakers' historic reverence for life. As I explored the serene campus, I felt this attitude emanate out from it like a healing aura. I easily saw why Quaker William Penn was the only colonial governor reputed to enjoy peace and harmony with the native Americans.

I quickly discovered the solitude of the nearby woods, a place of incredible healing beauty. Walking meditatively along the path by the creek, encompassed by flaming reds and golds, I knew hours of utter ecstasy. "Am I still on the earth or have I died and gone to heaven?" I mused. *"Or, are the two one? I am surely in the blessedness of eternity now!"* It was an auspicious beginning for a remarkably rich year.

To Pendle Hill's strong spiritual and intellectual foci, I was able to make a contribution with my bodywork therapy. This kept me grounded and also spilled over with benefit into the whole community. I earned most of my spring quarter tuition giving massages and even teaching wholistic massage to some classmates who requested that training. Gradually, I began doing healing therapy with persons outside the community, some coming to me from quite a distance. I smile to recall the day that unexpected recognition came my way from the surprised Pendle Hill administrator. He'd just learned that one of my regular clients was a very generous, long-time Pendle Hill benefactor, a man who'd recently discovered help for his serious health problems on my massage table. So the dignified administrator knocked on my door requesting a wholistic massage experience for himself!

I knew with certainty that this was the place of multi-dimensional teaching Michael had seen. In addition to bodywork, I had opportunities to share the light of my mind. I led an off-campus series for women from the greater Philadelphia area who came to explore Psyche's heroic journey of feminine individuation with me. It was one of the largest and most stimulating groups I'd led, and reflected my own growing maturity.

I spent hours of solitary bliss immersed in my books on feminine psychology. And I fed from the shared quiet of daily worship and the bustling activities of a meaningful community life. A nourishing sense of family developed among us there.

Even so, I ached for a primary relationship that winter. My woman's need to share a warm closeness with a man went unmet. I noted with frustration that the attractive men were either married or much younger than I.

Then I hit a whole new layer of mourning related to Len. (Divorce is indeed a process rather than an event.) My earlier "selective memory" of the ways my marriage violated my growing personhood had been necessary to getting free. And I was still angry, in touch with yet another layer of previously buried indignation. But now I was also inundated by memories of Len's fine qualities, of the things I'd cherished in him that I would cherish in any man, of much we'd meaningfully shared over twenty-five years. How I missed just having him for a friend with whom I could occasionally sit down and chat! I wept copiously as I processed these sharp feelings of loss.

I was obviously still doing my grief-work—a painful, continuing task which I could not avoid if I wanted to be whole.

> *I believe one has to return to one's past, not once but many times, in order to pick up all the threads one has let fall through carelessness or unobservance.*
>
> *I believe above all one has to return again and again to weep the tears which are still unshed. We cannot feel all the grief of our many losses at the time we suffer them. That would be too crippling. But if we would really gather our whole lives into a single whole, no emotion that belongs to us should be left unfelt.*[2]

Even as I was present to those stormy emotions I lifted them up for transformation, often as a sheer act of will. I frequently affirmed—whether I felt it or not: *"Len, in the power of my Divine Self, I love you; I forgive you; I thank you for all you taught me; I release you to your highest good in God."* Progress was very slow.

I was paying my dues for the new reality pattern Michael had said I'd stabilize into that year. In my worst hours it was only his prediction of a "powerful relationship" awaiting me somewhere out there that kept me going.

And I did feel that subtle new reality. Here no one had ever known me as anyone but Helene Joy; I'd dropped tons of ballast from my past. I experienced the respect Michael had predicted, and continued to courageously carve out an autonomous sense of myself. When I felt alone and scared I'd head for the woods to cry my tears, to regain my inner strength.

The deepest loneliness came at Christmas. Only two of us students had no place to go during the holiday break. My daughter, Lynn, lived only six hours away, but the door to her home was no longer open to me. This was to be another baptism through pain.

52

Sacrificing My Child

*It is . . . the unspeakably painful struggle of a woman
to separate from her possessive emotions, the struggle
which alone can give birth to love.*[1]

Helen M. Luke

It almost seemed like a cruel cosmic conspiracy. Not only did
Lynn break contact with me, but Rolf moved back to the west
coast as I moved east. Clark was intensely involved in medical
school and a romantic crisis in the midwest. I was to face the trial
of my first Christmas without family.

I joined Pendle Hill's maintenance staff for the three vacation
weeks to pay for my extra room and board. Keeping hard at work
was a great blessing. But those nights I sobbed myself to sleep,
past caring whether anyone heard my anguish or not.

There were many reasons for Lynn's action. For one, her insecure and therefore possessive young husband insisted upon it.
(How easy to spot possessiveness in another!) He'd been threatened by our closeness from the beginning, and my move to the
east coast alarmed him. But ironically, it was a woman who most
influenced Lynn's action. She was a charismatic, self-styled spiritual teacher toward whom Lynn and her husband were gravi-
tating, a woman who seemed the very incarnation of Divine Love.
But in time she instructed those idealistic young people in her
group to break all contact with "old energy"—including parents.
She gradually pulled a tight curtain of secrecy around her flock,
exhibiting the dark will to power of many cult leaders. Using
flattery and her keen, almost magical gifts of intuition, she pro-
gressively took mind-control over those young people in ruthless
disregard of their personhood.

In the pain of being separated from my children (for Rolf later
joined himself to the group) I was again forced to confront the
demonic potential of a woman's unconscious if she loses touch
with her inner feminine principle. This woman began to see herself as "all Goodness, all Love, all Light," as the infallible mouth-
piece of Truth to her disciples. As she refused to recognize and
take responsibility for her shadow side, it acted destructively.
Tragically, she lost her human warmth and the saving grace of
humility as her ego became inflated with a sense of her power to

control others. And her unconscious identification with the all-powerful goddess finally robbed her of her earlier power to love.

These influences were coming to bear upon Lynn at a time when she legitimately needed to make her declaration of independence from me, her biological mother. For she had a right to claim title to her own life, and our ways of expressing womanhood seemed to have drastically diverged. Lynn had married at eighteen, had her son at nineteen, and now at twenty was relishing a brief taste of security with her own home and family. All this, just when I was setting forth alone, teaching and embodying the heroine's transforming journey. I'm sure it was the last thing she wanted to confront.

"We'll be inviting you for Christmas only if it feels right," she'd said kindly but firmly.

That was the last time I heard from my beautiful daughter for over three years. (I had no assurance that I would *ever* see her again.) Neither of us consciously knew it, but she was soon to be catapulted onto her own lonely path. She would lose everything precious to her, and she had to go through that dangerous passage from innocent maidenhood to conscious womanhood without my support. Perhaps someday her gripping tale shall also be written.

But I feel quite sure that in some unfathomable way the mother-daughter mysteries were still operative between us. Helen Luke, commenting on the Demeter-Persephone myth which illumines these mysteries, says that only when a woman will accept the painful Demeter experience is she strong enough to consent to life's thrusting her child (inner or outer) into the transforming fire.[2]

So gradually I made sense of my pain through my studies. I learned that a woman who presses toward maturity purges her love of every bit of possessiveness.

> *Possessiveness destroys the true Eros in women. It is the subtlest of all the dangers when we give our love. . . . This then is the Great Offering . . . she is willing to risk the loss of a relationship rather than make possessive demands upon the person loved.*[3]

I discovered that the need for a woman to "sacrifice the son" is a universal, archetypal theme. In my case, it applied to both daughter and sons. This letting go is necessary in order that both mother and child be free to fulfill their respective destinies.

> *. . . the mother's instinctive identification with the
> "fruit of her womb" must be broken if she is not to
> destroy her son's right to his own life. . . . The "sac-
> rifice of the son" is one that has always been de-
> manded of the mother. It must be made in progressive
> stages from the moment of the child's birth up to the
> time when he reaches manhood . . . But profound
> transformation of an instinct can be achieved only
> through discipline and at the cost of much conflict
> and suffering. . . . Her need to be herself, to become
> whole, is opposed to her subservience to the mother's
> instinct.*[4]

This was obviously the next step in my woman's journey. Life
was insisting upon a deeper letting go of my children. I would
now serve them, and myself, best by attending one-pointedly to
the step-by-step path of my own wholeness. With this understanding I not only surrendered to my pain; I embraced it as yet another
purifying fire leading me to true inner freedom.

But the loneliness of that relinquishment, plus the longest,
grayest, bone-chilling winter I'd ever known, caused my spirit to
burn dangerously low at times. I kept putting one foot in front
of the other, crying out for the warmth of spring in my heart.

> *We must go on living. We must emerge from this
> totally self-centered, self-pitying sorrow and be awake
> to other people. We must work, we must relate, but
> we must not deny our grief.*[5]

So, day by day, the transformative process continued within
me. And when spring did finally blossom forth in glorious pro-
fusion, there was but a lingering ache where the searing pain in
my heart had been.

53

"Come Beloved; My Arms Are Waiting"

The feminine is the unitive. Every important synthe-
sis I had in my thinking was brought about by a
dialogue with a woman.[1]

Teilhard de Chardin

When my transformative year at Pendle Hill ended, I knew
only that I was not yet to return to California. I felt rather lost,
in fact. But again the Spirit went before and prepared the way,
and some generous friends in Maryland lovingly opened their
home to me while I got my bearings. It was there that I connected
with that "powerful relationship."

Things often do seem darkest before the dawn. The whole summer had passed by, leaving me feeling confused and unproductive.
One night I poured my burdens into my journal:

> *I hesitate on the threshold of this next chapter of my*
> *life. Do I want to put forth the effort to create work*
> *here? Where will I find the energy to begin again?*
> *Perhaps I'm just deluding myself, thinking I have a*
> *future. Tonite I'm feeling deep empathy with the*
> *world's lost, tired, discouraged, poor, suicidal. God,*
> *don't let me ever forget how awful they feel.*

Was I Psyche of the myth, losing heart before the enormity of
my next developmental task? Psyche had learned that regression
is impossible when the very river in which she tried to drown
herself frustrated her attempt. Again it seemed that I, also, had
come too far to turn back.

By fall I began to see some light at the end of the tunnel. My
hostess suggested some women I might contact for a group, and
soon I was again teaching a women's series.

This time I called it "The Second Defloration," reflecting my
own growth in loving.

> *The beginning of her love was a marriage of death*
> *as dying, being-raped, and being-taken; what Psyche*
> *now experiences may be said to be a second deflora-*
> *tion, the real, active, voluntary defloration, which she*

accomplishes in herself. She is no longer a victim, but
an actively loving woman.[2]

As I prepared for that group, I again became aware of my powerful yearning for a beautiful man with whom to share my new capacity for loving. The symbolism of Psyche's lamp, which earlier in my journey felt burdensome, now excited and inspired me:

> *The symbolism of the lamp in the myth points to the light-bearing capacity of women. . . . Feminine light is exquisitely beautiful. . . . It is the Jewish custom for the woman to light the sabbath candles on Friday evenings. . . . It is she who begins the sabbath; she who provides the light.*
>
> *A woman has the capacity to show the value of her man with the lamp of her consciousness. . . . Terrible things happen to men who are deprived of the presence of women, for apparently it is the presence of women that reminds each man of the best that is in him. . . . There seems to be a peculiar vacant spot in a man's psychology here. Most men get their deepest conviction of self worth from a woman, their wife or mother, or, if they are highly conscious, from their own anima. . . . The woman is the carrier of evolution for him in one way or another. She sometimes lights him into a new kind of relationship. The man is terrified of that, but he is equally terrified at the loss of it . . . he depends on the feminine light more deeply than most men are willing to admit.*[3]

I had experienced that phenomenon during my romantic relationship with William. Indeed, he'd once told me, "You are the light of my life." And I'd been astounded to watch him come alive during our love affair. Now I was yearning to once again share my love-light with a man, and on a deeper, more complete level.

One night the intensity of this desire awoke me from sleep in the pre-dawn hours. I found myself urgently sending forth from my heart this spontaneous, poetic call:

> Come, beloved, for I have warm, strong feminine
>   energy to bestow!
> The oil in my lamp is bountiful and burning
>   brightly.

118

Let it light your way to greater consciousness;
Let it fire you awake to layers of yourself which
    lie waiting to be discovered,
To treasures you've never dreamed are within you.
I need to give you my feminine light.
I need to receive from you your loving masculine
    energy.
Oh man of God, I need to give. I need to receive!
Come, O worthy one; my arms are waiting.
You who are ready, come—and may the Divine bring
    you!
I am ready, my beloved.
My arms are open and waiting.

(from my journal)

In just five short days, a beautiful man named Pete answered that yearning call of my heart.

54

The Next Big Step

As you get your independence, you want to share it.[1]
Gabrielle Roth

"Everything's been a progression and you're ready for the next big step," Michael had told me a year before. I was truly ripe! And so was Pete.

We met at a single's workshop in Columbia, Maryland one evening when I responded to an inner nudge to go there. But as I looked around at the several men present I wondered why I'd felt the drawing to come. Then, one hour late, in slipped Pete.

I didn't know how deeply I'd be stirred by this short, gray-haired man with the gentle manner and merry eyes. But I knew that I felt comfortable with him immediately. After the meeting, over a cup of tea, we found we shared much in common. He'd been divorced for several years and during much of that time had hoped to marry a particular woman who'd kept him dangling. He was finally saying "Forget it!" to her about the time we met. He, too, was in his late forties and had grown children. He was the son of Quaker parents and had recently begun a sincere spiritual search. Of course he knew about Pendle Hill.

Pete lost no time in pursuing me full speed. I loved it! The next morning after we met he called me to suggest an all-day outing. "Where would you like to go?" I'd been dying to visit the Smithsonian museums in Washington, and what a happy day we had there. He called me again the next day and the next and the next. His career as a college biology teacher gave him most afternoons free. Ornithology was his specialty, and we spent many magical hours with binoculars in the forest and at the seashore as he opened to me the wonderful new world of birds.

Pete's masculine ego was more secure than any other man I'd been close to. This was apparent in many subtle ways; for instance, though I was an inch taller than he, this bothered him not at all. When I finally indicated my readiness to share with him sexually, I found him skilled, sensitive, and *very* passionate. And I was amazed at my own passion! The goddess of love was alive and well in me, fusing my earth instincts with my spirit into ecstatic moments of fulfillment.

I was needing a place to live but was not earning enough to support one so his invitation to share his townhouse was timely. Such living arrangements were popular in that ávant-garde community. After a few weeks deliberation, I was surprised at how natural I felt moving in with him.

I found an enormous, consistent tenderness in my heart for this dear man. Just to see him or hear his step on the stairs evoked a sweet warm-pudding sensation in the center of my chest. I admired his capability as a man in so many areas. And I loved feeling cherished and protected, able now to put at ease the courageous independence I'd carved out at such great cost. I joyously reconnected with the feminine principle at my center, home of my spirit. I welcomed my man taking charge, often asserting his gentle authority, allowing me to lean on his strength and be present to matters of the heart. I knew a deep exaltation as I entered into loving union with this man, reflecting his beauty as the moon reflects the sun. How delightful to find I could relax into this loving interaction without feeling that I was losing myself, for Pete respected my personhood apart from him—as did I! Giving myself to him, receiving what he gave to me, was soul-satisfying beyond anything I'd ever experienced.

I recalled with greater comprehension Michael's earlier words, "The last thing Christ wants you to do is to deny your fulfillment as a woman, for it's through your womanhood that you'll realize your spiritual nature. Your body is the temple . . . "

Our relationship produced dramatic growth in both of us, especially a new burst of creativity. Pete brought forth inspired beauty through his nature photography and his enthusiastic green thumb in the garden. And *now* I felt ready to begin my work again.

> ... *I have yet to meet the woman who did not know in her heart that love is her main concern and that the secret of her success in any field was her personal love in the background.*[2]

I gradually developed an enjoyable, unhurried practice in bodywork-counseling. I was amazed to find myself working at a whole new level of proficiency, and word got out that people were having significant breakthroughs in my therapy room. Other health professionals in the community began referring their clients to me for deep emotional discharge and transpersonal healing sessions. I became meaningfully involved in the expanding lives of some very special people.

"This will be one of the most creative periods of your life, with that beautiful masculine energy backing you up," a wise friend and colleague predicted. She was right. Pete's supportive presence in my life lifted my spirits and empowered me.

It seemed to follow naturally that unusual recognition began coming my way. First, my wholistic work was written up in the local newspaper. Then several months later I received a call from the Baltimore Sun. Their medical-topics reporter had been trying for months to interview a doctor who was using holistic approaches in his practice but was "too busy" to grant an interview. When the frustrated reporter saw the announcement of some lectures I was to give on "Wholistic Healing" at Baltimore's Sinai Hospital (co-sponsored by the extension office of Pete's college), she asked if she might do a feature on my work as a wholistic counselor. It was another case of being in the right place at the right time!

The resulting half-page article gave me unaccustomed new visibility and respectability. Under my picture, the caption read, "Helene Joy's clients want to be whole." Yes, she'd captured the essence of my life's purpose: catalyzing wholeness.

Now other opportunities to teach and lead workshops opened before me. Never had I felt so fulfilled in my work! Nor had I known such a healing love relationship with a man. How beautifully the Spirit had gone before and made the way plain.

55

"He Lets You Be Who You Are"

Mutual service without betraying one's own deepest truth is the paradox at the very centre of the art of living.[1]

Irene Claremont de Castillejo

Pete and I were so glowingly happy and harmonious, we soon began talking about marriage. Then we agreed that we'd know better after a year together whether to take that serious step. But we already felt like mates. So we had to face the challenges of intimacy.

The deepest form of personal crisis for a woman may be to find a balance between independence, both physical and psychic, and interdependence.[2]

My need for lots of breathing space, for personal freedom, came up quickly. One night as Pete held me snugly close to him in sleep, I dreamed I was at a meeting where I was to give an important speech but couldn't get to my feet to deliver it because someone had an arm-lock on me! Remembering how stifled I'd felt in my marriage to Len, I felt compelled to ward off any clutching, conscious or unconscious. As I explored that with Pete, he admitted that he had a lot of security needs already invested in our relationship.

"This time I'm playing for keeps," he'd told me with an engaging grin on our third date.

"But you attracted me as a loving partner," I reassured him. "If I should leave, you could attract another woman just as desirable."

He courageously struggled with that idea for a few days. And the moment he reached a resolution, I felt a weight lift off both of us. Not long afterwards he laid a beautiful card on my desk which read, "We cannot own each other. We cannot change each other. We can only discover each other. . . . I love you. Pete." I was deeply touched.

Even so, I later found myself saying to him, "As soon as I am able, I must contribute toward the rent. I just can't allow myself to feel like a 'kept woman.' " And still later in the year I told him,

"If we marry, I'll probably keep my own name." It was a measure of his maturity, I thought, that he did not seem at all threatened.

My fierce determination to retain my autonomy showed me how much I'd chafed within my quarter-century, patriarchal-style marriage—a marriage in which "the two become one and the husband is that one." I had felt more violated than I realized.

"Pete lets you be who you are," an astute friend observed with appreciation. It was true. What a gift! Now that I was able to bring a sense of self to a relationship, I'd attracted a man secure enough to respect that hard-won autonomy. This meant, of course, that we could have a real relationship rather than a mere symbiosis. I was continually amazed that I could love and support this man without feeling like I'd sold myself out.

Even as my greater wholeness was reflected in these dynamics, vestiges of old patterns showed their unwelcome faces. One of them was my fear of letting myself be loved.

> *If her marriage is cut short, leaving unresolved problems . . . she will continue to bear the burden of an unfinished relationship which will crop up to be dealt with at every point in her life whenever she comes close to a man. It will become a kind of ghost which she can exorcise only through working out that problem which her release from her first husband left unsolved.*[3]

The very sweetness of my life with Pete brought up those residual fears of receiving love. When my skin allergy flared up and stubbornly persisted, I sought out a trusted, highly intuitive colleague for her perceptions.

"Your skin is saying: 'Don't touch me—I might love it, I might want more!' " she suggested.

"I was afraid that might be the message. But consciously I want to be touched, to be close."

"Yes, you're going to have to feed some new information to your subconscious." Then she pointed out soberly, "Your pattern, Helene, has been to try to control your relationships; that's a defense mechanism which says: 'As long as I'm in control, you can only get inside my heart as far as I'll let you.' Receiving love is very difficult for you; yet you give to so many, so you get unbalanced. Now this beautiful male polarity is here to help you learn to receive. Pete's going to break down a lot of your heart's barriers."

"Yes, I can already feel that happening."

"Well, he's awakening all kinds of new energies in you. Don't block it! Just let it happen! He has a way of uplifting you that you're not used to. Know that you're worthy of it!" I felt how hard it still was for me to feel worthy.

Then she underscored, "There's no need to fear this relationship based on a past one. Pete is quite different!" I could see she was right about that, though it seemed almost too good to be true. She encouraged me to accept his love without fear, to enjoy it. But she sensed that I was still troubled by something I couldn't articulate. Finally, she hit the nail right on the head. "Don't deny yourself, fearing that you might lose your life's purpose if you yield to your desires. You've come much too far along the path for that."

Thus reassured, I relaxed considerably and was more able to flow. Still, often aware of my thorny conflict between wanting to be loved and fearing to be hurt, I realized my inner child had never heard, "You're loved, you're cherished; it brings you joy." Pete was helping me discover that happiness. But as much as I yearned for it, I could not totally accept it. I was a house at least partially divided against itself.

I spotted other old patterns, as well. Sometimes I caught myself giving Pete double messages, a painful reminder of my life with Len. But now I was quicker to go off and confront myself in my journal, and to lift those patterns up for transformation.

This was the powerful relationship Michael had foretold. Powerful obviously did not mean easy. Love had stirred me to depths of vulnerability I didn't know I had; I was frightened and confronted; but, more than anything, I was amazingly fulfilled.

56

"Hell No, I'll Not Go"

The presence of God is a disturbing presence, especially when His voice is as close to us as our nightly dreams.[1]

John Sanford

My heart yearns to tell you, "We lived happily ever after." But my tale has no value to me or to you unless it is scrupulously honest.

I'd been with Pete not quite a year when I had my first dream portending change. I recorded upon awakening: "I am finishing college and it's time to start packing boxes to leave. But I'm dismayed to find I've not completed my biology course and have to meet a tight deadline in writing my term paper. I cannot graduate till it is finished."

I was sure the biology course referred to my life with Pete since that was his field. The dream troubled me. And a few weeks later I had a similar one: "I've finished college and I'm packing to go home. This time I have a clear sense that everything has now been completed."

Now I was assailed by incredible self-doubting. "Do I lack the maturity to remain in a relationship after the honeymoon intensity has passed? Am I unable, after all, to be close to a man? Am I once again neurotically judging my man, feeling as I now do that I'm growing at a much faster rate than Pete? Does my preoccupation with non-attachment spring from my fear of commitment and intimacy? Perhaps I don't want to acknowledge how important a caring, protective man is to me. Have I already forgotten how lonely and unproductive I was before Pete powerfully entered my life?"

"Hell no!" I journaled one night. "I'm not relinquishing his mellow companionship just because he doesn't measure up to my ideal image. I'll *not* leave Pete unless the Spirit clearly says 'Go!' And that's that."

But the Spirit within was already directing me through my dreams and now even my waking thoughts. One evening I looked at dear Pete during dinner and calmly realized, "I cannot stay here the rest of my life."

I quickly beat down such thoughts whenever they arose. At no time in my whole life had I felt so cherished, so protected—like I'd finally reached a fruited oasis after a long, lonely nomadic journey. No wonder I resisted letting go and resuming the path.

But now my body joined my thoughts and my dreams in alerting me to the necessity for change. My skin's rashy inflammation worsened until it covered half of my body. I was miserable with itching and profuse sweating, robbed of much of the joy that my work and love-life should have afforded. I knew from previous such massive skin outbreaks that medicine was not the answer. So I turned to traditional (wholistic) Chinese acupuncture since there was a fine clinic in our community.

During those months of treatments, I was constantly stirred up emotionally. Old cans of worms seemed to open inside me. My nights were restless with dreams of haunting, forgotten scenes from my childhood, and the reoccurring traumatic theme of the death of my marriage. They were filled with abandonment, with unspeakable sadness, with feelings of fury. Obviously there was still a deep wound in my heart. "Emotionally burned," my skin seemed to be screaming; "I've got to break out!" I'd awaken from fitful sleep in anxiety and reach out for Pete to hold me close. I was humbled to see how much I needed him, for I was more vulnerable now than ever.

Except for his loyal, loving companionship, I could not have entered into that season of deeper purgation. But his caring presence also helped catalyze that creative crisis. Much later I could see that he was the very embodiment of the mellow, nourishing side of my father—the side I'd reached out for largely in vain because Dad had typically hidden his love for his little girls under his tense, scolding exterior. It was the safety I felt with Pete that allowed more of my early primal pain to come to consciousness.

But my skin trouble persisted. Through it all, I continued to faithfully journal, meditate, and record my disquieting dreams, honoring the intuition that "the way out is the way through."

During that tumultous period, I drew inspiration from "New Dimensions"[2] and "New Horizons"[3] radio interviews which William occasionally sent me on tape from California. How I needed to be fed from the mindstream of those on the leading edge of change! I was often homesick for the San Francisco Bay area where so much of the new age consciousness was being birthed.

In the summer of my second year with Pete, my son Clark and his wife invited me to join them for a vacation in Michigan. It was the opportunity I'd been looking for to meet Jungian author Helen Luke. I called her Apple Farm community near Kalamazoo and got permission to spend two days there. In preparation for that long anticipated visit, I gathered the dreams I wanted her to help me interpret—plus a host of questions about my puzzling, complicated life.

By now I was feeling subtle pressure from Pete's increasing desire to marry. But I was caught, unable to say "yes" or "no."

It was the perfect season for a journey to the wise woman I admired so greatly.

57

Journey To The Wise Woman

Woman cannot and should not separate herself from the Mother; her freedom lies in her increasing consciousness of how this image lives itself within her own psyche. . . . The image [of Earth Mother] takes on various aspects as woman penetrates its meaning . . . as instinct, as conscious love, and as spirit that penetrates into the heart of love itself. The spirit form of the Earth Mother is the "Wise Woman," who knows the secrets of the heart.[1]

Francis G. Wickes

"Do you love him?" she asked me several times as her eyes searched my face.

"I do," I honestly replied.

"Yes, you'd not live with a man at your age unless you love him. From what you say, he would feel more secure if you'd marry him, and since you love him you may want to give him that gift."

But I needed to explore with her my uneasiness about his hang-ups.

"There are no perfect men," she smiled wisely. "The only place a woman can find the ideal masculine is within her own consciousness. When she finds that within, she can relate to a man much less conscious than herself and meet him where he is. Are there areas in which you admire Pete as a man?"

"Oh yes, many." I willingly told her about them. "But he sometimes gives his power away to women a little like my ex-husband used to do."

"Well, men often do this. You're up against a collective problem, not just a personal one. You're describing the charming, charismatic 'Puer Aeternis' (eternal youth) who lives out his feeling side through his woman. . . . There just are no ideal men out there, and you've been looking for one before making a commitment in marriage. Can you love him just as he is? Part of a woman's function is to lovingly awaken her man to greater consciousness," she reminded me.

I remembered with chagrin the impassioned call of my heart which had attracted Pete in the first place: "Come, beloved, I need to give you my feminine light." At some point I'd let up on the giving and slipped into judging. Any illusions I had about my power to fully love suddenly shattered. I'd had a partial transformation, to be sure. But I had not arrived!

> *She . . . blossoms in the Spring, but the long summer which follows is a very slow ripening process with nothing much in the woman herself to show for it.*[2]

As though to underscore the message of my previous dreams about completing college, I had a similar one my second night at Apple Farm. Helen was most interested in this fresh one which I had to share with her the following morning.

"I dreamed of a young man now grown and ready to leave home. Was it for higher education or the military? I am his mother, preparing him spiritually as I stand with my arms raised in reverent salutation to the Great Spirit, demonstrating how to invoke its light and protection. I feel great sadness as my son prepares to leave home; yet I release him with my blessing as he embarks upon his next stage of life."

"Your dreams are most encouraging," she said. "Something in you has come of age. Some things are ready to be left behind, such as, perhaps, an adolescent hope of finding the perfect man. . . . I like that part of you which commends your fine, young son-self to the Spirit. Yes, it is the finest, the best within us, which must be offered. It was Christ, the perfect one, who was the sacrifice."

She continued encouragingly, "Your dreams indicate that things are working themselves out. Sometime soon I'd expect you to be ready to make a commitment to Pete *or* a clean break. Just wait until you become so uneasy that you *have* to make that decision; you will most certainly know when that time comes." I felt more disturbed than cheered by that prediction, and needed to ask Helen more about her own life. I wondered, "Has she known loneliness? Has she known pain?"

I'd immediately been attracted to her pretty, apple-cheeked face framed by her modish, short gray hair. About eighty, she was a study in aliveness, obviously fulfilled in her life as a counselor and writer. Yes, she said in response to my questions, she had been married and had a family in her native England. But during World War II her husband had fallen in love with a younger woman who stayed in London with the men to save the city. When he wanted to marry the other woman, Helen had released him with love and understanding, yet not without the inevitable period of mourning. Eventually she left England to begin her work as a Jungian counselor in the United States. She had studied personally with Carl Jung, who'd foreseen her eventual move to America years before it came to pass! Her loving wisdom had attracted searching people to her, and a group of women now lived with her at Apple Farm as an extended family, dedicated to living consciously and sharing their light with the many guests—both men and women—who gathered there.

Helen had obviously paid her dues and she'd come through with her spirit undampened. So I really listened when she told me how Apple Farm women were finding fulfillment in directing the creative (sexual) energy into developing "the interior life." I could see what creative people they were, and marveled that they were finding wholeness apart from the energization of primary relationships with men. Perhaps for the first time that way of life seemed to me viable.

But I had to own my fears, for I had a vague sense of choosing that path in previous lifetimes as a nun with only mediocre success. I mused, "I have a strong need to express my love through emotional and sexual intimacy."

As though reading my mind, she immediately offered, "Of course, if one can have a loving relationship with a man, that is preferable, I think."

When I rejoined Clark for a few more vacation days at the lake, he noted my thoughtful preoccupation. I was sobered by the things Helen had revealed to me about myself even as I was also grateful. I sensed she was right about another, imminent turning point on my unfolding Path.

58

Forcing My Own Hand

Affairs are now soul size.[1]
Christopher Fry

"You will know when it's time to make a commitment or a clean break," I recalled on the plane back to Baltimore. My fiftieth birthday was only a few months away.

Pete brought me home from the airport to a house that was spotless and shining, with one of his fragrant bouquets adorning the table. This dear man always seemed to say with such finesse, "You are my queen. I honor and cherish you."

"How blessed I am," I realized afresh. "This is my man, my

129

home. So marriage *must* be the right course . . . "

For a week I did not mention that possibility to him. Instead, I inwardly affirmed many times, "I love him just as he is." He felt that silent acceptance and responded. Our love-making held very special tenderness. "Perhaps I'm ready to experience unconditional woman-man love for the first time in *all* my lives," I journaled, greatly encouraged.

But during the day while he was at work I gave in to the need to just space out. I collapsed in front of the TV, drawn especially to Star Trek reruns. Captain Kirk's brave adventures in other realities fed my freedom-loving soul as I inwardly sorted and processed.

After a few days I began forcing my own hand, edging up to the subject of marriage as I told Pete about Helen Luke. I wondered why he didn't seem more delighted. In retrospect, I know he was intuiting my ambivalence, for even as I said, "I'd like to make a commitment to you," my energy was incongruent.

"Well," I reasoned with myself, "I'm still afraid of commitment. So what's new? I can't let that fear run my life forever. If I know myself at all, I'll do better with a husband for the rest of my life than without one. And Pete is the most desirable candidate I see anywhere around."

I called Clark to see if he could find a weekend to fly in for our wedding. ("You bet, Mom.") And I called my sister for her blessing. ("Absolutely, Sis.") I wrote to Nan and Rob in California, and suddenly found myself begging them, "Please pray for me. People are supposed to be happy when they're getting married, but I feel like I'm dying inside. Pray that my feelings catch up with my decision."

By now Pete was seeing the seriousness of that decision, and with my encouragement he happily told his children and close friends of our plans to marry.

It was only after we looked at possible places for the wedding that I began to hesitate. At every place the way had seemed blocked. Finally I got quiet and acknowledged sorrowfully in my journal, "The way *is* blocked. I cannot proceed further until this heavy feeling of resignation turns to peace or joy." Reluctantly, I shared that with Pete. He looked worried.

The next day I impulsively dialed my pastor-friend, John, and his wife in California. I poured out my troubles to them. "I'm planning to marry a fine man here in Maryland but something's not right. Can you help me get some guidance?"

They called back after a long hour of listening prayer. "Honor your hesitation," they quietly suggested. "We sense that it's coming from the highest level, from your soul."

"Oh, John and Anna," I suddenly wept. "I don't think I'd have the energy to start all over again. This man loves and cherishes me, and I love him. He makes more money than I could ever dream of earning. He offers me the security and the freedom to be myself which I've always needed from a man . . . "

"Oh God *bless* you, dear Helene," John exclaimed. Compassionate tears choked his voice as he softly added, "If anyone in the whole world deserves happiness, it is you."

59

Letting Go Again

The rhythm of time is . . . known to woman. . . . The feminine unconscious responds to this rhythmic movement [of the tides]. . . . Woman cannot command these tides . . . [but] she learns the moment of the tide's turning. . . . She learns the rhythm of pain and gladness that beat like waves upon her heart. She learns that love is joy and sorrow, fulfillment and renunciation, and that at the last, love becomes what she herself has made of it.[1]

Frances G. Wickes

John and Anna poured on the prayer-power. I could tell, for I was buoyed up with an incredible energy which coursed through my body like pulsating ocean waves. I felt lovingly upheld, able now to relax enough to get the guidance I needed.

That night I wrote in my journal, "I am willing to stay and love Pete with an open heart if that is my Highest Good. I'm willing to leave and face the demons of fear and loneliness if that is my Highest Good. The inner Presence that guides my life has *never* led me astray. Praise to my God-Self who melts my heart open and directs my Path of loving. . . . Thou knowest, Thou ordainest. So be it."

Then I lay awake till almost dawn, awash with relief and gratitude. In the morning I stepped refreshed into the living room, and immediately I knew the answer. For I experienced seeing the room through the reverse end of a telescope—far away, diminutive, detached from me. I perceived it as "Pete's home," no longer "our home." And with that came peace.

I could not have relinquished Pete and all that he represented without the absolute certainty that I could *not* stay. I had to enter with sincerity into those wedding plans. I had to test my soul's purpose—to urgently ask, "Is there *no way* this can be?" I had received my answer.

"Stay on your Path," Michael had once told me. "Follow your own sense of where you feel most vital and alive." Now I remembered how he'd also said, "I see you in the east from one to three years." It was now exactly three years.

Pete and I wept together. Then he went alone to the seashore for several days to seek strength and solace. He found them! As I sent him love along our strong telepathic connection, I felt him returning it and lovingly releasing me. It felt clean, without bitterness, confirming the stature of this man whom I'd been privileged to call "my beloved" for two unforgettable years.

60

I Return

To leave the old when it no longer sustains our growth, to bid farewell with gratitude to the forms which held us once, and to turn with excitement to the new expression of life now called for by our deepest self—this is the challenge of life.[1]
University of California workshop

Once again I was driving my faithful Blue Angel, now retracing the route of my spiritual journey three years before. I wept a lot the first couple of days; I was already missing Pete dreadfully. But my heart also sang in celebration of the rich fruits of my sojourn in the east. I now felt so *seasoned!* I'd tested my powers, pushing my limits out beyond where I had dreamed they could go in both career and in love. I had discovered a lot about myself—what I am, what I am not. I just had to admire this plucky gal who'd come so far from her shaky beginnings.

"I am nothing if not an adventurer," I realized. "Once again I've assented to the misty creative void rather than the known or secure." A long sigh escaped me.

Mile after mile across America the beautiful (truly, my eyes and heart feasted upon it), my worthy old car served as my chapel, filling with spontaneous songs and prayers of thankfulness. On the last day, as I crossed from Nevada into California, I noticed my foot getting heavy on the gas. Yes, I did feel like I was coming home! But to whom or to what? "Lord, just send me to some people who need me," I found myself breathing.

I felt soul-weary, too. Again I asked the familiar question, "Do I have the courage, the energy to start over?" I reflected on how my faith had grown through the years. "Has not the Red Sea parted for me several times over? Have I not proved the timeless truth: When one is on her true Path everything in the Universe backs her up?" Lost and weary as I felt, I knew not to despair.

Like a homing pigeon, I now headed for John and Anna's church. I rang the doorbell, and oh-so-gratefully fell into the warm, brotherly embrace of William who'd been told of my imminent arrival and wanted to be the first to greet me. As he and I and John and Anna shared a joyous reunion dinner that evening, I knew I'd find the courage to make it. What a gift, spiritual family like this! It was as though we'd never been apart. But to their questions about my future I could only answer, "I don't know. And that's scary."

My sister had moved from Hawaii to Berkeley, so I gratefully headed for her comforting hospitality. While there, one of her friends whom I scarcely knew asked me, "Where are you going next?"

"Up to the Sierra foothills to visit some dear friends. After that, I have no idea."

"I have a vacant camping trailer parked up near that area," he said. "If you should ever want to use it, let me know and I'll get it to you." I pondered the meaning of that kind, unexpected offer.

A few days later I headed for Nan and Rob's ranch. Again, a loving reunion! "If only you had a trailer," they generously suggested, "you could park it over the hill on our east forty and stay there indefinitely."

"Oh my goodness, I've just had the offer of one!" How could I doubt that the Spirit had again gone before and prepared the way?

And so I returned to the nourishing bosom of Mother Earth to complete my lonely grief-work for Pete and to get my bearings.

> *. . . it is very painful, but very important, for women to realize and accept their loneliness . . . Living in the forest would mean sinking into one's innermost nature and finding out what it feels like. . . . The forest*

*is the place where things begin to turn and grow
again; it is healing regression.*[2]

It took three months for that blessed renewal to occur. I lay
naked in the warm, autumn sun each day until its healing rays
cleared the last vestiges of my two-year skin affliction. Among
the great, wise oaks I journaled, I meditated, I wept. I hiked, I
picked wild blackberries and gleefully splashed in the creek. I
felt a renewed connection to all growing things.

The anticipation of turning fifty shook me up some. What an
age to be starting all over again! But my birthday proved lovely
and untraumatic; William drove up to take me to a nearby Mother
Lode town for a quiet celebration dinner. Nan and Rob were wonderfully supportive, as always.

As the unusually mild autumn began to turn to winter's chill,
I found my heart restored, ready to take the next step toward
more active life.

> *Frequently the way of the heroine involves a consid-
> erable time of withdrawal from the world, which for
> us means introversion, when she must go apart and
> endure the suffering of silent waiting for the time of
> her deliverance . . .*[3]

The time of my deliverance had come. I felt at peace. And now
I knew where I was to go.

61

Cosmic Trouble-Shooters

> *For it is surely a lifetime work
> This learning to be a woman
> Until at the end what is clear
> Is the marvelous skill to make
> Life grow in all its forms.*[1]

May Sarton

I had awakened in my trailer in the forest one morning with
the urgent thought, "I'm to be at John and Anna's church by New
Year's Day." It felt like my next cosmic trouble-shooting assignment.

I should explain to you that seer Jack Schwarz had told me ten years before, "An important part of your life's purpose is to function as a cosmic trouble-shooter." After he explained that spiritual vocation to me, I became more aware of my uncanny penchant for dropping into situations just ripe for resolution, seemingly awaiting my arrival. Or I happily found my mere presence catalyzing another's personal expansion, both within and outside of my scheduled counseling "duties." How grateful I was to realize that my greatest service to the world consists of those very activities which fill me with enthusiasm and joy! "All God wants us to be is ourselves."[2] I loved the excitement of the cosmic trouble-shooting role *except* where I was resented as a boat-rocker! (After my divorce, I suddenly found I was threatening to insecure husbands who feared my influence upon their wives.)

When I recognized that Life had called me to function as a human catalyst, I yearned to attain this pure Taoist ideal—still so far beyond my reach:

> *The great of earth*
> *How softly do they live,*
>
> ....
>
> *One hardly knows that they are there,*
> *So gently do they go about their tasks*
> *So quietly achieve;*
> *When they have passed,*
> *Their life's work done,*
> *The people look and say:*
> *It happened of itself . . .* [3]

Now, after my healing time in the forest, I was ready for my next trouble-shooting assignment. So at the earliest opportunity I asked John and Anna to pray with me, to check out this latest intuitive nudge.

"Yes!" I was to join their ministry, to help their inner city church through a time of major change and relocation. It was not an easy task, but was eventually a successful one. And I did receive the blessing of appreciation there.

During my year at the church, William again became my best friend and my champion. I continually marveled at the loyalty of this good man. I had left him, I had caused him hurt; yet here he was, backing me up once again. True, he was now much more guarded emotionally than before. I felt sad about that—and deprived, too. There was an aching emptiness in my heart where Pete's love had been, and I wanted William to try to fill it. But he was a different person; his strengths lay elsewhere.

As I worked through that disappointment, I was forced to turn deeper within for that nurturance. (Eventually, I would find the grace to thank William for that.) Now I sought out a collegue for an amazing, close-to-the-core experience of inner healing.

Any woman committed to wholeness must return to her inner child again and again to peel off the layers of wounding. If she needs help, she is wise to seek it whatever the cost. I had done that many times, and now I was ready for the most gentle, most effective surgery of all.

62

Little Girl, I Love You

. . . the human nervous system cannot tell the difference between an "actual" experience and an experience imagined vividly and in detail.[1]

Maxwell Maltz

"If you see your mother getting it, you'll believe that you can get it too," Eve told me.

The "it" was the devoted, cherishing love of her man which melts a woman's heart and brings happy tears to her eyes. Again, I was feeling painfully bereft of that.

We began that healing-of-memories session with a relaxation procedure, then Eve's instruction: "Picture a little girl. Tell me her age and the expression on her face."

I flashed on a snapshot of myself at age two. "Oh my, her face is like a thundercloud!"

"O.K. Remember, now, part of you remains safe here in this chair. Now imagine the soft, nurturing, motherly part of you going to this child and giving her the opportunity to tell what she's feeling. She's had so many heavies in her life, telling her what she *should* and should *not* feel, but nobody's let her express what she *does* feel. Get this child to tell you the truth. You'll have to imbue her with a lot of love and white light to get her to trust you . . . "

True; that scowling, yet precious child hesitated awhile before moving into my outstretched arms. Then, as she laid her head and body limply against me, I felt how sad, how utterly dispirited this little girl was. "More dead than alive," I thought with tears smarting behind my eyelids. It was some time before we could go on.

"What's the thing she wants most right now?" Eve asked.

"Loving masculine nurturance."

"O.K. First she needs to see her mother get it . . . Take this little girl into the kitchen and seat her on your lap by the table. Mother is cooking. Father comes in and we see him go over to his wife and stand beside her. He hasn't said a word yet, but you can feel how he's so proud of her; she's such a good cook, taking care of him and their little child. He raises the pot lid, sniffs the food, and slips his arm around her waist. See him tell her how much he loves her, and he's so thankful that she's there."

Though only once had I seen Dad give Mother that kind of open, loving appreciation (on their fiftieth wedding anniversary), I'd fortunately met a few men in my life who did demonstrate that wonderful energy. So I could imagine the scene Eve suggested, especially as she reminded me, "We're making magic now." I loved making magic!

Then I spontaneously saw my mother respond to Daddy's love; she sighed deeply and laid her head tenderly on his shoulder. Then she looked at him with happy tears sparkling in her eyes. My heart was warmed to see my young, pretty Mama basking in the love of her man.

Eve continued, "And now she turns and looks at you through her tears, and for the first time she recognizes you for who you really are; how blessed she feels to have given birth to this wise, beautiful being sitting there."

"Now," she continued, "allow both parents to come over and hug you. The hugging is expansive! You feel very forgiving, very loving, very healed as you feel their energy touch yours. There's no longer a need to pull back or hold in." Yes, I could begin to feel that, thank God.

As we closed the session, she reminded me, "Now feel your oneness with your own larger, nurturing part, the angel-, the madonna-you. That's where your power and your wholeness come from." I was grateful for her reminder; I could not expect any man to be source of that for me.

If her essential being is defined by love and her vul-
nerability is so great, then the male is doomed to fail.
He can never love her enough; he can never fill her
up; no man, no child can fill that crying, empty space.
The image of woman as a devouring monster, swal-
lowing the male into its own depths, that we find in
traditional mythological images such as the Medussa
and the Gorgon may come from man's experience of
woman as insatiably dependent upon him for her very
being.[2]

I listened to the tape of that session and another similar one
with Eve many times until the image of a happier, loved little
girl began to "take" in my consciousness. Then I began returning
to that growing girl in spontaneous meditations as I sensed which
memories needed my transforming madonna-touch. I am far from
finished. But this has made a subtle, yet powerful difference in
the way I relate to every part of my life.

63

Sword Of The Feminine Spirit

There is a new breed emerging . . . the peaceful war-
rior of the heart . . . positive change-maker.[1]
Danaan Parry

As I completed my year at the church I did not see a clear next
step. I sorted out my thoughts one night in my journal. "Lending
my energy to that ministry was important . . . but what destiny
really brought me back to California?" How I wished I could find
Michael!

Obviously I was to find my own answers now. (The true teacher
knows when to stay away as well as when to appear.) I tried to
be patient even while straining hard at the bit. Gratefully, I
entered back into the rich consciousness stream of the San Francisco Bay area, home to my expanding spirit and birthplace of so
much profound human metamorphosis. And now I participated
in all this at a new level of maturity, with some basic, necessary
experiences as a woman lived out. The wholeness process continued deep within me.

One day I felt inspired to create a personal-goals poster. (In

New Thought teachings this is sometimes called "treasure map-ping.") I began with one main thought: "It's now the season to create for myself some prosperity! I choose to claim the Abundant Life materially as well as spiritually!" Coupled with that, I yearned for greater self expression—a larger, more significant use of my talents.

As I searched through magazines and brochures for pictures, then cut and pasted, a fascinating thing happened. The poster seemed to take on a life all its own. Excited, I finally stepped back to see what I'd revealed to myself thereby.

There were images, indeed, of things I desired: a new, economy car to replace the Blue Angel, a healthy infusion of dollars into my bank account. But the main focus turned out to be the people I'd placed around the photo of myself, *all midwives of the spirit.* Here beside me was a picture of Marilyn Ferguson whose best-seller, *The Aquarian Conspiracy,*[2] had quickened my pulse with its hopeful vision for our world's future. Next to her was Margaret Mead, pioneer among women who have contributed to an under-standing of the whole. There was Jean Houston, new age educator, brilliant evocateur of *The Possible Human.*[3] Dr. Helen Caldicott was there; she's one of my heroines because of her mobilization of the "Physicians for Social Responsibility" who so effectively address the insanity of nuclear war.[4] Mother Theresa was there, saintly yet tough madonna of the planet's downtrodden. And be-side her I'd put Mother Mary with the Divine Child she lovingly brought forth to transform human experience. There was also Barbara Marx Hubbard, futurist and inspiring teacher of hu-manity's upward spiritual leaps.[5]

There were some fine men as well: Carl Jung, Willis Harmon, Robert Müller. But basically my poster had become a sampling of women consciousness warriors—women who've courageously and creatively stepped forth to help us through this precarious passage in our planet's history, to build new models for a better tomorrow.

My heart skipped a beat as I took this all in. "Am I finally glimpsing the goal of my long heroine's journey? And many of my sisters' journeys as well?" Aha! I could see that my higher Self had known it all along!

> *—the moment is upon us when victory will hang upon*
> *the readiness of women to confront the most powerful*
> *of all the dark forces ranged against us—that which*
> *no man can conquer with his sword, that which is*

vulnerable only to the newly found sword of the fem-
inine spirit.[6]

64

"What Is My Part Of The Whole?"

It is the crucial moment for every woman who is dri-
ven by the creative spirit into the Logos world. Will
she imitate man, in which case her spirit will turn
sterile and daemonic; or will she, in the midst of her
intoxicating freedom, be true to her basic nature? . . .
[Eowyn's] hand which wields the sword of her spirit
is wholly a woman's hand.[1]

Helen M. Luke

"My contribution will surely be less public than these sisters
on my poster," I journaled. And that felt O.K. "But I *must* share
my creative gifts, however modest. Mine must be some necessary
piece of the Whole." I could feel how despair would surely destroy
me if I didn't find a way to express them for I simply wouldn't
survive the anguish of watching my creative spirit wither and
die. Urgently, I asked, "What *is* my part?"

Seven years before Michael had spoken of a book I would someday write. "Save all your journals; you'll need them. Your writing
will be important to women breaking free from patterns you've
been so stuck in," he'd told me unflatteringly.

"Am I now ready to share my naked, gutsy tale?" I wondered.
"I've not yet completed the journey. I'm only halfway up the mountain!"

"Begin," I felt intuitively. "The writing is the next part of your
journey."

> *Through her book the child which was her true self*
> *was conceived and would in time come to birth and*
> *maturity.*[2]

Indeed, this writing has given identifiable form to the new
birth. I have collected the scattered threads of my life and woven
them into a rich, living tapestry. It has taken four very patient
years. For I've had to pause many times to do unfinished grief-
work along the way. And to frequently push through the heavy,
self-defeating patterns which will probably always challenge me.

And I've needed time to behold the metamorphosis of this new woman I found gradually emerging before my astonished eyes.

How can I encapsulate for you the treasures of my journey thus far?

First, I think of what I learned from Mary. Communing with her spirit while the prayer candles flickered, I was moved by the beauty of her receptive devotion as she lovingly brought forth her Divine Child in joyous obedience to her soul's purpose. At her feet I consciously said "Yes!" to fulfilling my own unique destiny. Every cell in my body sang the "Hallelujah Chorus"!

So my journey has been about reconnecting to my feminine nature from which I'd been so painfully estranged. It's been about opening and softening, yielding, forgiving myself and others. About uncovering the healing love that was already inside me, and taking that love back to my half-dead inner child who waited to be resurrected. It's been about choosing the vulnerable beauty of my woman's heart whenever I caught myself retreating fearfully behind old "macho" defenses. And I've sorted seeds, discovered a lot of my own deeply held values, faced my darkness, been as honest with myself as I'm able to be.

The journey has required the healing and positive development of my strong masculine side which was fighting for a chance to meaningfully express—and insisting that this animus power serve me, back me up, in obedience to love.

Especially the journey has been about letting the deprivation of my past be the *very springboard* into my life's fulfilling purpose. Speaking of another heroine whose natural femininity lay buried for long years while the sword of her spirit was being forged, Helen Luke writes movingly:

> . . . *this mirrors the predicament of many women in this century. Born into a family in which, perhaps, the father has succumbed to the softness of his anima, while the mother, as mother, is simply absent, since she is buried in a mass of animus opinions, the daughter is brought up without a clear image of either masculine or feminine, while all around her the decay in the collective . . . consciousness presses in upon her . . .*
>
> *What has been the effect of all this on women of great potential warmth and nobility? Like Eowyn they grow up determined to face the battle on the masculine level, fighting with all they have for a cause*

or an ideal, or, at the opposite pole, succumb to . . . an indiscriminate instinctual sexuality which, cut off from relationship, ends by destroying Eros itself. Nevertheless there are not a few who come, as did Eowyn, through suffering and courage, to find their wholeness as women . . .

. . . then indeed she may come at infinite cost to confront and destroy that [cruel king of dark despair] who yields to no power but that of the true woman who has dared to grasp the sword of the spirit.[3]

Oh! When our hearts yearn to embrace this saving task, we must faithfully tend the sacred fires within. I am learning (oh yes, still learning) to intuitively wait upon my God-Self in receptive devotion, then to step forth in trusting obedience to my inner rhythms. To hone these abilities, I've been led beyond the church of my birth into the practice of meditation and the study of metaphysical principles. I'm learning to juggle paradoxes! I continue to synthesize the spiritual and the psychological, and the East and West. Perhaps I've already come full circle, for the mysteries of Christian symbolism now nourish me more deeply than ever before. I'm learning to root these healing images in my Earth Mother connection, which, in turn, is giving rise to my inner Wise Woman "who knows the secrets of the heart."

I must not fail to tell you that my journey's been about a moment-by-moment transformation from victim to choicemaker. It's still very much about finding the sacredness of my own selfhood, and never, never losing it again.

The heroine's journey is an individuation quest. Traveling this path, the heroine may find, lose, and rediscover what has meaning to her, until she holds on to these values in all kinds of circumstances that test her. She may repeatedly encounter whatever threatens to overcome her, until finally the danger of losing her selfhood is over.[4]

65

The End Is Goddesshood And Joy

Your joy is your sorrow unmasked.
And the selfsame well from which your laughter
rises was oftentimes filled with your tears.
And how else can it be?
The deeper that sorrow carves into your being, the
more joy you can contain.
Is not the cup that holds your wine the very cup
that was burned in the potter's oven?[1]

Kahlil Gibran

Finally, I'm discovering that the heroine's journey is also about joy. How amazing to me that I'd taken Joy as my new surname several years ago while still reeling painfully in the cauldron of the refining fire! The guiding Mind could see then what lay ahead. For my struggles have now greatly eased, and I'm enjoying a quality of relationship to myself for which I've always yearned. It warms me from within like a steady, glowing flame. In those ecstatic moments when that flame leaps high, I find my heart burning in a passionate love affair with Life.

Synchronistic with this growing inner joy have come many expressions of it outwardly. I am wonderfully rich in loved ones. Beautiful son Clark, already launched in a promising medical career, and warm, lovely Lynn are my true friends in the finest sense of the word. Having both carved out their own personhood to an admirable degree, they love and respect me without being in awe of me. I deeply respect and enjoy them, appreciating the honesty with which we relate. I was almost overwhelmed by the incredible privilege of officiating, three years ago, at Lynn's marriage to her tall, new husband. This precious daughter whom I once was forced to relinquish, and in the fullness of time joyously regained, has added two delightful children to my life, a grandson and granddaughter. How privileged I was to participate in the awesome home birth of each! All that was tragically ripped from Lynn's arms during those years in the cult has been restored to her manyfold. (We are sad that son Rolf has not yet emerged from that cult and still remains in hiding. But we have hope, for the little group is gradually disintegrating as the young people mature and reclaim title to their own lives.)

For the past four years my dear friend and spiritual brother, William, has shared his quiet home with me so I could gestate and give birth to my book. With great devotion he has protected my privacy to create, staying in the background, believing in me, refusing to give energy to my discouragements along the way. Once again, though differently than before, he has been a mainstay through all kinds of weather.

My heart is full of promise as I step across this new threshold in my life. My eagerness to share the new birth is attracting opportunities so to do. Who knows where this cosmic troubleshooter may find herself in the fulfilling days ahead?

As my joy increases, I again feel kinship with Psyche's archetypal journey toward wholeness:

> *What happens at the end of the myth? Eros and Psyche are reunited . . . on Mt. Olympus, and Psyche bears a daughter named Joy.*[2]

Because of Psyche's heroic, step-by-step movement through the dark underworld passage and into the light of consciousness, she has earned her place beside her beloved Eros on a higher level of loving union. Michael had thrilled me with that possibility years before. ("But you must walk out of hell . . . into the light . . . alone.")

Psyche's heart is fully a woman's heart, with her animus power developed and tested by the demands of the journey. Through her lonely labors of rebirth—and with the strategic aid of her matured god-mate, Eros, at the end—she has transformed from mortal womanhood to true goddesshood. She has fulfilled her birthright, her destiny!

And the child of her wholeness is a girl, symbolizing the birth of her own real self. Joy, I am reminded, is always the fruit of that inner mystical union of feminine and masculine, of Earth and Heaven, which is wholeness of being. Psyche has truly won.

And Psyche is everywoman of the heroic Way.

> *When a woman finally reaches her full development and discovers her own goddesshood, she gives birth to . . . joy.*[3] *. .*

And she cannot help but share it! Joy is a natural gift from the heart of such a woman, and every living thing bursts forth into blossom in her unpretentious presence. She evokes beauty, faith, love. She is an initiating center of life.

Dear sisters of the Journey, never has our despairing world so needed the living gifts that flow from a whole woman's heart. We are here. We are now. We must dare, *as women,* to grasp the sword of the Spirit and strike the root of that violence bred of fear which threatens to annihilate all we love.

And so we do, each finding our part.

Blessed are we among women.

CHAPTER NOTES

THEME PAGE

1. Helen M. Luke, *Woman: Earth and Spirit,* New York, Crossroad, 1981. p.4.

PREFACE

1. Archetype is defined as a universal pattern or template of the human psyche, found in all cultures through observing their myths, fairytales and dreams. These universal themes have great power to grip us. Some frequent archetypal symbols: hero/heroine, the wise old man/wise old woman, the goddess, the nourishing/devouring mother, the Divine Child, the eternal youth, death/rebirth.

2. See Erich Neumann's treatment of this fairytale in his *Amor and Psyche, The Psychic Development of the Feminine,* New York: Princeton University Press, 1956; and, Robert Johnson's *She,* King of Prussia, PA: Religious Publishing Co., 1976.

3. See Helen M. Luke's treatment of Eowyn, J.R.R. Tolkien's heroine from *Lord of the Rings,* in her *The Way of Women, Ancient and Modern,* Apple Farm, Inc., 12291 Hoffman Rd., Three Rivers, MI 49093, pp. 1-9.

1.

1. Jean Shinoda Bolen, *Goddesses in Everywoman,* San Francisco: Harper and Row, 1984, p.1.

2. Helen M. Luke, *The Way of Woman, Ancient and Modern,* Apple Farm Community, Inc., 12291 Hoffman Rd., Three Rivers, MI 49093, p.1.

3. Kahlil Gibran, *The Prophet,* New York: Alfred A. Knopf, 1952, p. 16, 17.

2.

1. Roberto Assagioli, *Psychosynthesis,* New York: Hobbs, Dorman & Co., 1965, p. 49.

2. Helen M. Luke, *Woman: Earth and Spirit,* New York, Crossroad, 1981, p. 11.

3. Marie-Louise von Franz, *The Feminine in Fairytales,* Spring Publications, Inc., Dallas, TX, p. 27.

4. May Sarton, *The Lion and the Rose,* New York, Rinehart & Co., 1948, p. 60.

5. "Amor and Psyche" is an example. See Erich Neuman's treatment of the tale in his book *Amor and Psyche, The Psychic Development of the Feminine,* New York, Princeton University Press, 1956. Also, see Robert Johnson's *She,* King of Prussia, PA 19406, Religious Publishing Co., 1976.

3.

1. Ernest Holmes, *How to Use the Science of Mind,* New York: Dodd, Mead & Co., 1950, p.v.; and, Ernest Holmes, *The Science of Mind,* New York: Dodd, Mead & Co., 1966, p. 30.

2. Spoken by Lisa deLongshamp, Wingsong Growth Center, 450 Santa Clara Ave., Oakland, CA 94610.

3. Helen M. Luke, *The Way of Woman, Ancient and Modern,* Apple Farm Community, Inc., 12291 Hoffman Rd., Three Rivers, MI 49093, p. 27.

4. Alice Miller, *The Drama of the Gifted Child,* New York: Basic Books, Inc., 1951, pp. 8 & ix.

5. Karen Horney, *Feminine Psychology,* New York: W.W. Norton & Co., 1967, p. 56.

6. Helen M. Luke, *The Way of Woman, Ancient and Modern,* p. 22.

7. I started my study with a book about Edgar Cayce, *There is a River,* by Thomas Sugrue, available from the A.R.E. Bookstore, P.O. Box 595, Virginia Beach, VA 23451, and other bookstores.

8. Anne Rush Kent, *Getting Clear—Body Work for Women,* New York: Random House, 1973.

4.

1. Jean Beggs, "Chrysalis," publisher unknown.

2. Irene Claremont de Castillejo, *Knowing Woman,* New York: G. P. Putnam's Sons, 1973, p. 58.

3. Ibid., p. 58

4. Anima is defined as the personification of the unconscious femininity in a man; animus, the unconscious masculine side of a woman. While yet unconscious they often manifest negatively, destructively in a person's life. But discovered and related to, they become a positive enrichment to the whole individual.

5. Ruth Bebermeyer, *"Good Mornin', Pain"* is the title song from an album which I obtained from: Community Psychological Consultants, 1740 Gulf Drive, St. Louis, MO 63130. However, they have moved and left no forwarding address.

5.

1. Quoted from Erich Fromm, *The Art of Loving,* New York: Bantam

Books, 1963, p. 19, by Penelope Washbourn, *Becoming Woman,* New York: Harper & Row, 1977, pp. 59-60.

2. Again I refer you to Erich Neumann's *Amor and Psyche,* New York, Princeton University Press, 1956; and, Robert Johnson's *She,* King of Prussia, PA 19406, Religious Publishing Co., 1976.

3. Helen M. Luke, *The Way of Woman, Ancient and Modern,* Apple Farm Community, Inc., 12291 Hoffman Rd., Three Rivers, MI 49093, p. 30.

4. Marie-Louise von Franz, *The Feminine in Fairytales,* Spring Publications, Inc., Dallas, TX, p. 165.

5. John Sanford's lectures were given at St. Timothy Episcopal Church, San Jose, CA. Later I found some of these ideas published in his, *The Invisible Partners: How the Male and Female in Each of Us Affects Our Relationships,* New York, Paulist Press, 1980.

6.

1. Elizabeth Janeway, *Man's World, Woman's Place,* New York: Wm. Morrow and Co., 1971, p. 205. I found this quote in Penelope Washbourn's *Becoming Woman,* New York, Harper and Row, 1977, p. 83.

2. Marie-Louise von Franz, *The Feminine in Fairytales,* Spring Publications, Inc., Dallas, TX, pp. 105, 106.

8.

1. Marie-Louise von Franz, *The Feminine in Fairytales,* Spring Publications, Inc., Dallas, TX, p. 46.

9.

1. Helen M. Luke, *The Way of Woman, Ancient and Modern,* Apple Farm Community, Inc., 12291 Hoffman Rd., Three Rivers, MI 49093, p. 9.

2. Erich Neumann, *Amor and Psyche,* New York, Princeton University Press, 1956, p. 110.

3. John Sanford, *The Kingdom Within,* Philadelphia, J.B. Lippincott, 1970, pp. 151-153.

10.

1. Kahlil Gibran, *The Prophet,* New York, Alfred A. Knopf, 1952, pp. 19, 20.

11.

1. Edgar Cayce reading 3003-1. For information, write Association for Research and Enlightenment, P.O. Box 595, Virginia Beach, VA 23451.

2. Native American shaman Rolling Thunder, as quoted by Irving Oyle, M.D. in a New Dimensions Radio interview, 1979.

12.

1. Spoken by Eileen Caddy, co-founder of Findhorn Community, Scotland at a lecture in Palo Alto, CA., 1983.

2. Joel Goldsmith, *Parenthesis in Eternity,* New York, Harper and Row, 1963, p. 228.

13.

1. Irene Claremont de Castillejo, *Knowing Woman,* New York: G.P. Putnam's Sons, 1973, p. 119.

2. Spoken by Theodore Lyon, M.D., in a counseling session, Palo Alto, CA., 1970.

3. Jack Schwarz is a spiritual teacher and counselor of international repute. He is founder of the Aletheia Foundation, 1809 N. 99 Hwy., Ashland, OR 97520. See his book, *The Path of Action,* (New York, E. P. Dutton, 1977), among others.

4. To pursue the relationship between blocked energy centers ("chakras") and disease, I refer you to: Ken Dychtwald's *Bodymind,* New York, H.B. Jove, 1977; and, to work with unblocking, Bernard Gunther's *Energy Ecstasy,* Los Angeles, Guild of Tutors Press, 1978.

5. Helen M. Luke, *The Way of Woman, Ancient and Modern,* Apple Farm Community, Inc., 12291 Hoffman Rd., Three Rivers, MI 49093, p. 31.

6. Esther Harding, *The Way of All Women,* New York, Harper and Row, 1970, p. 77.

14.

1. Philip Zaleski, *"The New Age Interview: Elizabeth Kubler-Ross,"* New Age magazine, Nov. '84; published by Rising Star Associates, Brighton, MA 02135.

15.

1. Kahlil Gibran, *The Prophet,* New York, Alfred A. Knopf, 1952, p. 13.

16.

1. Roberto Assagioli, *Psychosynthesis: A Manual of Principles and Techniques,* New York, Hobbs, Dorman & Co., 1965, p. 50.

2. Richard Moss, *"Three Mountain Foundation"* newsletter, March 20, 1984, P. O. Drawer 1180, Lone Pine, CA 93545.

17.

1. Marie-Louise von Franz, *The Feminine in Fairytales,* Spring Publications, Inc., Dallas, TX. p. 67.

2. I structure the exercise this way: Women work in pairs, one standing in front of the other, both facing the same direction. The one in front role-plays the dominating animus figure, harshly swinging a weapon (plastic bat or newspaper sword) while speaking intimidating threats and clichés, especially to the significant men in this woman's life. The other woman of the pair, who is virtually hidden behind the animus-figure, represents her own woman-self, eclipsed by the negative animus who stands between her and her world.

At some point, she takes "him" by the shoulders, turns him around to face her, and speaks forth her objections to his taking over her life. She instructs him to get behind her where he belongs, to back her up with his strength, so she can relate to the world from her woman-nature, her truth and her tenderness. He then takes his place behind her, putting his hands supportively on her shoulders; his weapon now becomes a torchlight which he shines over her right shoulder to help illuminate her true Path. All the pairs work simultaneously, and each woman gets to play both parts, of course.

I model the exercise first with a volunteer partner, for it takes some courage to act the obnoxious, negative animus role. But I find the conversations the women have with their negative masculine selves are often original, very creative, and profoundly moving. For instance, a woman often firmly spells out to him her values, what she is uniquely about, what season of her life she feels herself to be in, so he can back her up more appropriately. For more insights which I drew upon in creating this exercise, see Irene de Castillejo's discussion of the animus in her *Knowing Woman,* especially Chap. 5. See also John Sanford's *The Invisible Partners,* above.

3. Robert Johnson, *She,* King of Prussia, PA 19406, Religious Publishing Co., 1976, pp. 33, 34.

18.

1. Esther Harding, *The Way of All Women,* New York, Harper & Row, 1970, p. 139.

2. Robert Johnson, *She,* King of Prussia, PA 19406, Religious Publishing Co., 1976, p. 29.

3. Erich Neumann, *Amor and Psyche,* New York, Princeton University Press, 1956, p. 76.

4. Ibid., pp. 79, 80.

5. Robert Johnson, *She,* p. 25

6. Erich Neumann, *Amor and Psyche,* pp. 76-80.

19.

1. "Shadow" is defined by Jungian authors as the dark, unwanted, rejected side of ourselves which conflicts with our conscious attitudes and ideals. The shadow qualities are not all negative, but may be potentialities the ego has avoided the responsibility of developing. Coming to

terms with one's shadow, unpleasant as that may often be, is requisite to wholeness. The shadow typically appears in dreams as the same sex as the dreamer.

2. David Hart, *The Psychology of the Fairytale,* edited by Harriett Crosby, Pendle Hill Pamphlet 210, Wallingford, PA 19086, 1976, pp. 18, 19.

3. Frances G. Wickes, *The Inner World of Choice,* Englewood Cliffs, NJ, Prentice-Hall, 1976, p. 212.

20.

1. Penelope Washbourn, *Becoming Woman,* New York, Harper & Row, 1977, p. 52.

2. Helen M. Luke, *Woman: Earth and Spirit,* New York, Crossroad, 1981, p. 6.

3.Lectures given at St. Timothy Episcopal Church, San Jose, CA. I refer you to John Sanford's *The Invisible Partners,* New York, Paulist Press, 1980 for some related discussion.

4. I suggest two sources to explore this further: Irene de Castillejo discusses Toni Wolff's model of four feminine archetypes on pp. 63-72 of her *Knowing Woman,* (New York, Putman's Sons, 1973). Also, Jean Shinoda Bolen illumines this subject in her *Goddesses in Everywoman,* San Francisco, Harper and Row, 1984.

21.

1. Helen M. Luke, *Woman: Earth and Spirit,* New York, Crossroad, 1981, p. 56.

22.

1. Marie-Louise von Franz, *The Feminine in Fairytales,* Spring Publications, Inc., Dallas, TX, p. 161.

23.

1. Penelope Washbourn, *Becoming Woman,* New York, Harper & Row, 1977, p. 71.

2. Peter McWilliams, *Come Love With Me,* 5806 Elizabeth Court, Allen Park, MD. 48101, Leo Press, 1976. I found his poem on a greeting card.

24.

1. Kahlil Gibran, *The Prophet,* New York, Alfred A. Knopf, 1952, pp. 16, 17.

25.

1. Robert Johnson, *She,* King of Prussia, PA. 19406, Religious Publishing Co., 1976, p. 29.

2. Erich Neumann, *Amor and Psyche, The Psychic Development of the Feminine,* New York, Princeton Univ. Press, 1956, p. 100.

26.

1. Fritz Kunkel, *In Search of Maturity,* New York, Charles Scribner's Sons, 1949, pp. 26, 35.

2. To the reader who wishes to investigate this beautiful system of transpersonal psychology, I recommend to you: Roberto Assagioli's *Psychosynthesis,* (New York, Hobbs, Dorman & Co., 1965); Piero Ferrucci's *What We May Be,* (Los Angeles, J. P. Tarcher, 1982); and, for a creative application of Psychosynthesis techniques to use with children, Eva Fugitt's *He Hit Me Back First,* (Rolling Hills Estates, CA, Jalmar Press, 1983).

3. Later I was interested to read that when a woman has broken the domination of her animus by lighting the lamp of consciousness and identifying him, he returns to the inner world where he acts as helpful mediator between her conscious and unconscious. In *She* I read: "When Eros returns to the inner world of Aphrodite . . . he is able to send Psyche help at critical times in her development by using natural, earthly elements such as the ants, the eagle and the reeds." (Robert Johnson, *She,* King of Prussia, PA 19406, Religious Publishing Company, 1976, p. 52.)

27.

1. Helen M. Luke *Woman: Earth and Spirit,* New York, Crossroad, 1981, p. 10.

29.

1. Helen M. Luke, *Woman, Earth and Spirit,* New York: The Crossroad Publishing Co., 1981, p. 7.

2. Rosemary Haughton, *Feminine Spirituality: Reflections on the Mysteries of the Rosary,* New York: Paulist Press, 1976, p. 15.

3. Luke 1:36 & 46, RSV.

31.

1. Kahlil Gibran, *The Prophet,* New York, Alfred A. Knopf, 1952, p. 19.

32.

1. Helen M. Luke, The Voice Within, New York, Crossroad, 1984.

33.

1. Ann Belford Ulanov, *The Feminine in Jungian Psychology and in Christian Theology,* Evanston, Northwestern University Press, 1971, p. 266. Ulanov credits Erich Neuman and his "Psychological Stages of Fem-

inine Development," for inspiration here.

2. Spoken by David Spangler at the "New Wineskins" Seminar, "Imaging the Future" Conference, Columbus, Ohio, 1978.

3. Helen M. Luke, *The Inner Story: Myth and Symbol in the Bible and Literature,* New York, Crossroad, 1982, p. 8.

34.

1. Helen M. Luke, *Woman: Earth and Spirit,* New York, Crossroad, 1981, p. 60.

2. Mel Krantzler, *Creative Divorce,* New York, Signet Books, 1975, pp. 225, 227.

35.

1. Irene Claremont de Castillejo, *Knowing Woman,* New York, G. P. Putnam's Sons, 1973, p. 108.

36.

1. Irene Claremont de Castillejo, *Knowing Woman,* New York, G. P. Putnam's Sons, 1973, p. 178.

2. Henry Reed, Association for Research and Enlightenment newsletter: "Face to Face", Vol. 2, No. 6, Box 595, Virginia Beach, VA 23451.

3. Frances G. Wickes, *The Inner World of Choice,* Englewood Cliffs, NJ, Prentice-Hall, 1976, p. 218.

37.

1. Betsy Caprio, *The Woman Sealed in the Tower,* New York, Paulist Press, 1982, p.22.

2. For an inspiring exploration into this affirmative prayer technique, I recommend Frederick Bailes' *Hidden Power for Human Problems.* Englewood Cliff, NJ, Prentice-Hall, 1957. I bought my copy at a Religious Science church.

38.

1. John Sanford, in an introduction to Robert Johnson's *He,* King of Prussia, PA, Religious Publishing Co., 1974, p.5.

2. See my recommendations for reading: chapter twenty-six, footnote 2, above.

3. Robert Johnson, *He,* King of Prussia, PA., Religious Publishing Co., 1974.

4. Ruth Tiffany Barnhouse, M.D. in her Foreward to *He* by Robert Johnson.

5. Herb Goldberg, *The Hazards of Being Male,* New York, Nash Publishing, 1976, p. 31.

39.

1. Betsy Caprio, *The Woman Sealed in the Tower,* New York, Paulist Press, 1982, p. 37.

2. For resources of this nature I suggest the fine literature of Religious Science and Unity churches, and the writings of Joel Goldsmith.

40.

1. Helen M. Luke, *Woman: Earth and Spirit,* New York, Crossroad, 1981, p. 20.

41.

1. Irene Claremont de Castillejo, *Knowing Woman,* New York, G. P. Putnam's Sons, 1973, p. 161.

42.

1. Ann Belford Ulanov, *The Feminine In Jungian Psychology and in Christian Theology,* Evanston, Northwestern University Press, 1971, p. 11.

2. Elizabeth B. Howes and Sheila Moon, *The Choicemaker,* Wheaton, IL, Theosophical Publishing House, 1977, p. 69.

3. M. Esther Harding, *The Way of All Women,* New York, Harper and Row, 1970, p. 68.

4. Marie-Louise von Franz, *The Feminine in Fairytales,* Dallas, TX., Spring Publications, 1972, p. 59.

5. Irene Claremont de Castillejo, *Knowing Woman,* New York, G. P. Putnam's Sons, 1973, p. 103.

43.

1. John A.Sanford, *Healing and Wholeness,* New York, Paulist Press, 1977, p. 81.

2. Betsy Caprio, *The Woman Sealed in the Tower,* New York, Paulist Press, 1982, p. 30.

45.

1. Joel S. Goldsmith, *A Parenthesis in Eternity,* New York, Harper and Row, 1963, p. 146.

46.

1. Rosemary Haughton, *Feminine Spirituality: reflections on the mysteries of the rosary,* New York, Paulist Press, 1976. pp. 1, 8.

2. Helen M. Luke, *Woman: Earth and Spirit,* New York, Crossroad, 1981, p. 27.

3. Frances G. Wickes, *The Inner World of Choice,* Englewood Cliffs, NJ, 1976, p. 257.

4. Catalog available from Pendle Hill, Wallingford, PA 19086.

47.

1. Robert Johnson, *She,* King of Prussia, PA, Religious Publishing Co., 1976, pp.54, 55.

2. Kahlil Gibran, *The Prophet,* New York, Alfred A. Knopf, 1952, p. 9.

48.

1. Irene Claremont de Castillejo, *Knowing Woman,* New York, G. P. Putnam's Sons, 1973, p. 116.

49.

1. Betsy Caprio, *The Woman Sealed in the Tower,* New York, Paulist Press, 1982, p. 25.

50.

1. Linda Schierse Leohard, *The Wounded Woman: Healing the Father-Daughter Relationship,* Athens, Ohio, Swallow Press, 1982, p. xx.

2. Marie-Louise von Franz, *The Feminine in Fairytales,* Irving, TX., Spring Publications, 1972, p. 103.

3. Betsy Caprio, *The Woman Sealed in the Tower,* New York, Paulist Press, 1982, p. 22.

4. See number 1, above.

5. Frances G. Wickes, *The Inner World of Choice,* Englewood Cliffs, NJ, Prentice-Hall, 1976, p. 261.

6. Helen M. Luke, *Woman: Earth and Spirit,* New York, Crossroad, 1981, p. 73.

51.

1. Helen M. Luke, *The Way of Woman, Ancient and Modern,* Apple Farm Community, Inc., 12991 Hoffman Rd., Three Rivers, MI 49093, p. 8.

2. Irene Claremont de Castillejo, *Knowing Woman,* New York, G. P. Putnam's Sons, 1973, p. 157.

52.

1. Helen M. Luke, *Woman: Earth and Spirit,* New York, Crossroad, 1981, p. 58.

2. Ibid., p. 62.

3. Helen M. Luke, *The Way of Woman, Ancient and Modern,* Apple

Farm Community, Inc., 12991 Hoffman Rd., Three Rivers, MI 49093, p.19.

4. M. Esther Harding, *Psychic Energy,* Princeton University Press, 1973, pp. 193, 194.

5. Helen M. Luke, *Woman: Earth and Spirit,* p. 60.

53.

1. I regret that I cannot give the source of this quote from Teilyard. I copied it into my journal years ago from what I believed to be a reputable workshop brochure.

2. Erich Neumann, *Amor and Psyche, The Psychic Development of the Feminine,* Princeton University Press, 1956, p. 79.

3. Robert Johnson, *She,* King of Prussia, PA., Religious Publishing House, 1976, pp.36-38.

54.

1. Spoken by Gabrielle Roth during a New Dimensions Radio interview, April 21, 1979. See note below for chapter fifty-six, number two.

2. Irene Claremont de Castillejo, *Knowing Woman,* New York, G. P. Putman's Sons, 1973, p. 154.

55.

1. Irene Claremont de Castillejo, *Knowing Woman,* New York, G. P. Putnam's Sons, 1973, p.124.

2. Penelope Washbourn, *Becoming Woman,* New York, Harper and Row, 1977, p. 57.

3. M. Esther Harding, *The Way of All Women,* New York, Harper and Row, 1970, pp. 154-155.

56.

1. John Sanford, *Dreams: God's Forgotten Language,* Philadelphia, J.B. Lippincott Co., 1968, p. 119.

2. For information about available tapes, write to New Dimensions Radio, Dept. K, P. O. Box 410510, San Francisco, CA 94141.

3. For information about available tapes, write to New Horizons Radio, c/o Shared Visions, 2512 San Pablo Ave., Berkeley, CA 94702; phone: (415) 845-2216.

57.

1. Frances G. Wickes, *The Inner World of Choice,* Englewood Cliffs, NJ, Prentice-Hall, 1976, p. 215

2. Irene Claremont de Castillejo, *Knowing Woman,* New York, G. P. Putnam's Sons, 1973, p. 149.

58.

1. Christopher Fry, "*A Sleep of Prisoners,*" Oxford University Press, 1951.

59.

1. Frances G. Wickes, *The Inner World of Choice,* Englewood Cliffs, NJ, Prentice-Hall, 1976, pp.222, 220.

60.

1. I found this statement on a University of California (Santa Cruz) extension workshop brochure in the mid-seventies.

2. Marie-Louise von Franz, *The Feminine in Fairytales,* Dallas, TX, Spring Publications, Inc., p. 85.

3. Helen M. Luke, *Woman: Earth and Spirit,* New York, Crossroad, 1981, p. 19.

61.

1. May Sarton, "My Sisters, O My Sisters," in *The Lion and the Rose,* New York: Rinehart & Co., 1948, p.60.

2. Robert Bitzer, minister of Hollywood, CA Church of Religious Science, made this statement at a workshop at the Tri-City Church of Religious Science, Fremont, CA, 1984.

3. Irene Claremont de Castillejo gives credit for this poem to Ruth Tenney, who based it upon a poem by LaoTze. (Pp. 124, 125 of *Knowing Woman.)*

62.

1. Maxwell Maltz, *Psycho-Cybernetics,* Englewood Cliffs, NJ, Prentice Hall, 1960, p. xi.

2. Penelope Washbourn, *Becoming Woman,* New York, Harper and Row, 1977, pp. 56-57.

63.

1. I found these statements on Danaan Parry's *"Warriors of the Heart"* workshop brochure; for information write to him c/o Holyearth Foundation, P.O. Box 399, Monte Rio, CA 95462.

2. See Marilyn Ferguson's *The Aquarian Conspiracy,* Los Angeles, J.P. Tarcher, 1982.

3. See Jean Houston's *The Possible Human,* Los Angeles, J. P. Tarcher, 1982.

4. See Helen Caldicott's *Nuclear Madness,* New York, Bantam Books, 1978.

5. See Barbara Marx Hubbard's *Evolutionary Journey,* Evolutionary Press, 2418 Clement St., San Francisco, CA 94121, 1982.

6. Helen M. Luke, *The Way of Woman, Ancient and Modern,* Apple Farm Community, Inc., 12291 Hoffman Rd., Three Rivers, MI 49093, p.4.

64.

1. Helen M. Luke, *The Way of Woman, Ancient and Modern*, Apple Farm Community Inc., 12291 Hoffman Rd., Three Rivers, MI 49093, pp. 5, 7.

2. Ibid., p. 30.

3. Ibid., pp. 4, 5.

4. Jean Shinoda Bolen, *Goddesses in Everywoman*, San Francisco, Harper and Row, 1984, p. 293.

65.

1. Kahlil Gibran, *The Prophet*, New York, Alfred A. Knopf, 1952, p. 35.

2. Jean Shinoda Bolen, *Goddesses in Everywoman*, San Francisco, Harper and Row, 1984, p. 294.

3. Robert Johnson, *She*, King of Prussia, PA, Religious Publishing Co., 1976, p. 89.